BOOK OF MORMON
THE BIGGER
PICTURE

BOOK OF MORMON
THE BIGGER PICTURE

SHELL ABEGGLEN

authorHOUSE®

AuthorHouse™
1663 Liberty Drive
Bloomington, IN 47403
www.authorhouse.com
Phone: 1-800-839-8640

Published by AuthorHouse   10/22/2012

ISBN: 978-1-4772-8240-3 (sc)
ISBN: 978-1-4772-8238-0 (e)

An Enlightening and Inspiring Commentary
on the Book of Mormon

*   *   *

"And it shall come to pass that the Lord God shall bring
forth unto you the words of a book, and they shall be the
words of them which have slumbered." 2 Nephi 27: 6

"And in that day shall the deaf hear the words of the
book, and the eyes of the blind shall see out of obscurity
and out of darkness." 2 Nephi 27:29

THE AUTHOR'S
PERSONAL NOTE

Even though I have read the Book of Mormon many times over the last forty five years, I never really saw the "big picture" until 2005 when President Gordon B. Hinckley challenged us to speed read the Book of Mormon from July until December of that year. After that wondrous and inspiring experience, and a great deal of personal study, I felt that the pieces of the Book of Mormon puzzle had finally started to fit together, and I started to see, if you will, the big picture.

I found that many members of the church, even after having read the Book of Mormon several times, still can not clearly distinguish between the story of Ammon before King Limhi, and the story of Ammon before King Lamoni. Though this may be of trivial importance compared to gaining spiritual knowledge and an overall sense of the true value of the Book of Mormon, I point this out as one among a great many examples of things that are unclear to the average Book of Mormon reader. The fact is, most readers do not have an overall understanding of how all the puzzle pieces with the myriad of characters and all their stories fit together. Consequently, I have felt a "gnawing quest", perhaps even some kind of a vague obligation to search out and make things clear that are unclear, to gather pertinent authoritative references, to dig out fascinating editorial comments by general authorities, and share my discoveries in a simple straight forward format with those of us who are not Book of Mormon scholars and don't really have the time to read lengthy detailed Book of Mormon reference books.

Any one, who walks in to a bookstore where LDS books are sold, will find dozens of references, supplements, and commentaries on the Book of Mormon, providing an almost overwhelming amount of information and interpretations. This book, in its conciseness and simplicity, isn't meant to be a scholarly reference, nor is reading this book meant to be a great theological experience. And most assuredly, it is not in any way meant to take the place of reading the actual Book of Mormon with the special spirit that it carries, but if I have done my job well, it will certainly help the average truly interested reader to see a bigger over-all picture and hopefully contribute greatly to the enjoyment and understanding of the Book of Mormon. I dedicate this book to my wife who has been an unfailing support.

Shell B Abegglen

BOOK OF MORMON
THE BIGGER PICTURE

The title of this book, "Book of Mormon: The Bigger Picture", effectively summarizes in a nutshell, what this book is about and its purpose. The heart of the book is a simple but adequate summary of Book of Mormon events and also a who's who, but the book is much more than a summary. It clears up those vague relationships, events, and timelines, that sometimes confuse Book of Mormon readers, and may even lose them as they are led on detours by Isaiah, Zenos, and Zeniff. It is a stand back view, that trims the profusion of Isaiah quotes, the protracted allegories, the lengthy speech of King Benjamin, the eloquent and profound preaching of Alma and Amulek, and the spiritual soliloquies of Mormon and Moroni. Though all of the above spiritual passages are of great value, they can be studied later in depth, after the reader has gained an overall view of the continuity of the Book of Mormon story. This book connects the Book of Mormon story to the Bible story, historically, genealogically, and spiritually. It contains quotes from BYU professors and Book of Mormon researchers, from Parley P. Pratt and Oliver Cowdery's personal witness, and from the Encyclopedia of Mormonism, all to help the reader see a much bigger picture, and most importantly, it emphasizes that Joseph Smith translated The Book of Mormon through divine help, but that he did not write it.

This book was written with the intent to put the Book of Mormon in a whole new light of understanding for the average reader, so that they can see a bigger picture. People who were introduced to the book during its writing, said that it is just the kind of book that they have been looking for; just a simple guide and explanation to the Book of Mormon.

Shell B. Abegglen

CONTENTS

CHAPTER ONE

*   *   *

THE BIGGER PICTURE

Anyone who picks up the Book of Mormon to read it for the first time, cannot possibly perceive the possibilities in the journey they are about to take. Once one has had their heart and mind enlightened by its amazing accounts of courage and faith, its profound spiritual messages, its numerous miraculous events, its ancient historical authenticity, and its devout overall intent of being another testament to Christ, one can never fully go back to a life which is void of the spiritual force and influence of the Book of Mormon. Unfortunately people who pick it up with a certain amount of prejudice and skepticism being unduly critical, may be excluding themselves from an amazing literary and spiritual journey; a journey taken by literally millions of readers, a great many of whom gain an amazing life changing experience. President Ezra Taft Benson, the 13th president of the church, was widely known for his very strong advocacy of the daily reading of the Book of Mormon. He made this inspirational statement in 1986 at the October conference. "It is not just that the Book of Mormon teaches us truth, though it indeed does that. It is not just that Book of Mormon bears testimony of Christ, though it indeed does that, too. But there is something more. There is a power in the book which will begin to flow into your lives the moment you begin a serious study of the book." Millions of Book of Mormon readers can and will testify that this book is beyond the realm of the ordinary, and it truly does carry a special spirit with it that is simply unexplained by the usual rationale.

*   *   *

Because the Book of Mormon was composed by many ancient authors, written at different periods over a time continuum of more than a thousand years, there are some things about the Book of Mormon that can be confusing or at least seem complicated to the first time reader, or for that matter, even a regular reader.

This chapter is dedicated to pointing out a few significant items to remember while reading and studying the Book of Mormon. It specifies some important insights for seeing the bigger picture, and it emphasizes a most important relationship between The Book of Mormon and The Holy Bible.

IMPORTANT THINGS TO REMEMBER FOR UNDERSTANDING THE BOOK OF MORMON AND SEEING THE BIGGER PICTURE

*   *   *

INSIGHT # ONE: THE BOOK OF MORMON AND THE HOLY BIBLE ARE COMPANIONS, EACH OF THEM HAVING BEEN COMMANDED TO BE WRITTEN BY GOD WITH THE MAIN INTENT OF BEING USED AS "ONE IN TESTIMONY" TO THE DIVINITY OF HIS SON JESUS CHRIST. THEY ARE TOGETHER THE TWO STICKS REFERRED TO IN THE BIBLE

AS FOUND IN THE BOOK OF EZEKIAL, THE BIBLE BEING DESIGNATED AS THE STICK OF JUDAH WHILE THE BOOK OF MORMON IS REFERRED TO AS THE STICK OF JOSEPH OR THE STICK OF EPHRAIM.

Ezekiel 37:15-19

The Lord has always commanded his people to keep records. In the Old Testament, Jeremiah 30:2 says; "Thus speaketh the LORD God of Israel, saying, Write thee all the words that I have spoken unto thee in a book."

Then Ezekiel 37:16 commands "Take thee one stick and write upon it for Judah . . . then take another stick and write upon it for Joseph, the stick of Ephraim . . . and they shall become one in thine hand."

In 2 Nephi 29:11-12 the Lord makes it even more clear as to whom he commands to keep records. 29:11 "For I command all men, both in the east and in the west, and in the north, and in the south, and in the islands of the sea, that they shall write the words which I speak unto them . . ."

29:12 "For behold, I shall speak unto the Jews and they shall write it; and I shall also speak unto the Nephites and they shall write it; and I shall also speak unto the other tribes of the house of Israel, which I have led away, and they shall write it; and I shall also speak unto all nations of the earth and they shall write it."

Therefore, the Bible is certainly not the only record that the Lord has commanded to be written. In Second Nephi, the Lord says that in the latter days, fools will say, "A Bible, we have got a Bible, and we need no more Bible." (2 Nephi 29:6)

2 Nephi 29:8 "Wherefore murmur ye, because that ye shall receive more of my word? Know ye not that the testimony of two nations is a witness unto you that I am God, that I remember one nation like unto another?"

"2 Nephi 29:10 Wherefore, because that ye have a Bible ye need not suppose that it contains all my words; neither need ye suppose that I have not caused more to be written."

(see 2 Nephi 29:6-10)

As Latter Day Saints we study and revere the Bible, which is the "stick of Judah", that world-renowned written record of the Jews. In addition, we also study and revere the less known written record of the family of Lehi, who were the descendants of Joseph of old. This record of Lehi's descendants is called The Book of Mormon, "the stick of Ephraim", which is the written record of the seed of Joseph who was sold into Egypt. Joseph was one of the twelve sons of Father Jacob, the patriarch of the House of Israel. Jacob was the son of Isaac, and the grandson of Father Abraham, who was the grand patriarch of the House of Israel.

Who then was this Ephraim that the "stick of Ephraim" was named after? Even though he was the youngest son of Joseph who was sold into Egypt, Ephraim received the birthright from his Grandfather Jacob's hand; overriding Manasseh's traditional right as the eldest son. In Genesis chapter 49, the patriarch Father Jacob blessed his twelve sons and prophesied concerning their seed and the fate of the House of Israel. In verse 22, he prophesies metaphorically that his son Joseph would be a fruitful bough that would be separated from the rest of Israel going over the symbolic wall of the great sea so that his seed would be separated from their brethren. This prophecy was fulfilled when Joseph's descendants, Father Lehi and his family, actually did cross the great sea and so did become a fruitful bough in a new land, multiplying and eventually becoming two great nations in the Americas.

Lehi's sons and their Israelite wives unquestionably represented the fruit of Joseph who was sold into Egypt, through two different bloodlines. Although Father Lehi was a descendant of Manasseh, his own posterity would be descended through both of Joseph's sons. While Nephi and his brothers were the descendents of Joseph's son Manasseh, their wives had descended down through the lineage of Ephraim. See (Alma 10:3) as well as the footnote below:

*   *   *

James E. Talmage, Articles of Faith, p.504-505, Footnotes

1. Ishmael an Ephraimite—"The Prophet Joseph Smith informed us that the record of Lehi was contained on the one hundred sixteen pages that were first translated and subsequently stolen, and of which an abridgment is given us in the First Book of Nephi, which is the record of Nephi individually, he himself being of the lineage of Manasseh; but that Ishmael was of the lineage of Ephraim, and that his sons married into Lehi's family, and Lehi's sons married Ishmael's daughters, thus fulfilling the words of Jacob upon Ephraim and Manasseh in the 48th chapter of Genesis [verse 16]." :16 "The Angel which redeemed me from all evil. Bless the lads; and let my name be named on them, and the name of my fathers Abraham and Isaac; and let them grow into a multitude in midst of the earth."

—From "Discourse by Apostle Erastus Snow," at Logan, Utah, May 6, 1882, see Journal of Discourses, vol. 23, pp. 184, 185.

*   *   *

In 2 Nephi 3:5-12, Father Lehi is blessing his own sons and tells his youngest son, also called Joseph, that the Lord did promise Joseph who was sold into Egypt, that out of his loins, God would raise up a righteous broken-off branch out of the house of Israel. He also promised that their writings would be joined with the writings of

Judah, which would then come together to confound false doctrines and to bring this branch of Israel to the knowledge of their fathers and of the Lords covenants with them.

Today, we know this sacred record of the seed of Joseph, "the stick of Ephraim", as The Book of Mormon and it is venerated along with the Bible as another testament to the birthright and divinity of Jesus Christ, the literal Son of God.

In addition to Lehi's family, the Book of Mormon contains some of the record of the Jaredites who originated before Abraham, they having left from the tower of Babel when the languages were confused. It also records a brief history of the people of Mulek, who was the son of King Zedekiah in Jerusalem when it was captured and destroyed by the Babylonians in 587 B.C. The scriptures indicate that someday we will even have the records of the Ten Lost Tribes. see (2 Nephi 29:12,13)

These records have now all come together in our scriptures to enhance our knowledge of the Lords people and his dealings with them. They bring to us great wisdom and a spiritual energy that we can glean from reading and studying these ancient writings, as well as hope and faith. Nephi also points out an important warning that we are to garner from these writings for all men on the face of the earth. (2 Nephi 25:3) "Wherefore, I write unto my people, unto all those that shall receive hereafter these things which I write, that they may know the judgments of God, that they come upon all nations, according to the word which he hath spoken."

*   *   *

INSIGHT # TWO: THE BOOK OF MORMON IS NOT IN CHRONOLOGICAL ORDER. Like the Bible, the Book of Mormon is not a single book but a collection of books written by many authors, those authors of course, being ancient authors and prophets. Joseph Smith was a relatively uneducated, simple but inspired farm boy who translated it by divine power, but did not edit or rearrange the books. It was edited or abridged, and then all put together by the great military leader and record keeper, the prophet Mormon "according to the workings of the spirit of the Lord", hence the title; "The Book of Mormon." This was in about 385 A.D. towards the end of the thousand year Book of Mormon period, 600 B.C. to 421 A.D. His son, Moroni, made his own contributions, engraved the final entries, and then hid up these records for the next 1400 years until they would arise again from the dust for the benefit of the Lord's covenant people and the Gentile.

Therefore because there were many different writers and record keepers in the Book of Mormon, as well as the discovery of much older records many years after some historical records had already been written, not to mention other records that were lost from the chain of events, the happenings of the Book of Mormon are not always in a "sensible" chronological order.

The earliest historical period, the Jaredite period, took place many hundreds of years before Father Lehi and his featured family were even born, but the Jaredite history was not abridged by Moroni until the end of the Book of Mormon period and so consequently it was placed towards the back of the Book of Mormon in the Book of Ether. In contrast, later writings such as the "Words of Mormon", which were written towards the end of Book of Mormon times, were placed in the middle of the book by Mormon in order to connect the history on the small plates of Nephi to the history of the large plates of Nephi in an attempt to create some semblance of historical continuity. This all can be somewhat confusing, but is more evidence that Joseph Smith did not contrive the Book of Mormon, but only translated it. For a better understanding of the Bigger Picture, we will go more or less in chronological order in this book.

*   *   *

INSIGHT # THREE: THE RECORDS SHOW THAT ANCIENTLY THREE BOOK OF MORMON PEOPLES ARRIVED IN THE AMERICAS SEPARATELY AND AT DIFFERENT TIME PERIODS IN HISTORY. These three separate and totally different groups were the Jaredites, the Lehites, and the Mulekites. All of them came from the old world of the ancient Middle East and all three groups crossed the open seas and settled in the Americas, but all three at different dates. The adventurous Thor Heyerdahl, a modern day world-renowned explorer and archaeologist, made several ocean expeditions in order to prove that ancient people could have crossed the Atlantic and Pacific oceans on primitive rafts using the available ocean currents, and such an ancient people could have populated areas in the western hemisphere. Although Mr. Heyredahl was not necessarily trying to prove the authenticity of the Book of Mormon, he certainly did prove that the Book of Mormon peoples as well as others could have crossed the great seas to the Americas.

*   *   *

"Thor Heyerdahl (October 6, 1914, Norway—April 18, 2002, Italy) was a Norwegian ethnographer and adventurer with a background in zoology and geography. He became notable for his Kon-tiki expedition, in which he sailed 5,000 miles across the

Pacific Ocean in a self-built raft from South America to the Tuamoto Islands in the South Pacific.

In 1969 and 1970, Heyerdahl built two boats from Papyrus and attempted to cross the Atlantic Ocean from Moroco Africa to America. Based on drawings and models from ancient Egypt, the first boat, named *Ra*, after the Egyptian Sun God, was constructed by boat builders from Lake Chad using papyrus reed obtained from Lake Tana in Ethiopia and launched into the Atlantic Ocean from the coast of Morocco. After a number of weeks, *Ra* took on water after its crew made modifications to the vessel that caused it to sag and break apart. The ship was abandoned and the following year, another similar vessel, Ra *II*, was built of reeds and likewise set sail across the Atlantic from Morocco, this time with great success. The boat reached Barbados in the Caribbean, thus demonstrating that mariners could have dealt with trans-Atlantic voyages by sailing with the Canary Current across the Atlantic." (www.wikipedia.com)

*   *   *

The JAREDITES

Many hundreds of years before Christ was born, at the time of the "Great Tower", the people were so wicked that the Lord confounded their language and scattered them to the four winds. He preserved a righteous group under the leadership of a man that we know only as "The Brother of Jared", and sent them to a promised land in the Americas. Crossing the sea in barges, and after 344 days of open sea, they finally landed somewhere north of "the narrow neck" of land described in the Book of Mormon and they became a great civilization. (see Ether chapter six)

*   *   *

The LEHITES

In 600 B.C., Lehi, who was a righteous descendant of the Joseph who was sold in to Egypt, was inspired by the Lord to take his family, leave Jerusalem before its destruction, and to go into the wilderness. Led by the Lord, they were directed to a land of promise and sailed to the Americas. They landed south of "the narrow neck" of land, populating the area and eventually spreading northward, while dividing in to two main groups, the Nephites and the Lamanites.

*   *   *

The MULEKITES

In approximately 587 B.C., at the time of the Babylonian conquest and the consequential destruction of Jerusalem, Mulek, the only surviving son of the Jewish King Zedekiah, left Jerusalem with his group and they were "Brought forth by the hand of the Lord" to the Americas. The people of Mulek settled somewhere in the middle between the Jaredite landing in the North, and the Lehi landing to the South of the narrow neck of land. Leaving in somewhat of a hurry, they did not bring any records with them. Consequently, after hundreds of years, their descendants corrupted the language of the Jews until it was unrecognizable, not to mention that they also lost their religious heritage and their belief in God. They too populated the land becoming "exceedingly numerous", and they did establish the great city of Zarahemla under their King who was called Zarahemla. They would eventually merge with Lehi's descendants, who were the exiled Nephite group under the leadership of King Mosiah, the 1st.

Although members of the church often use the name "Mulekites", it is not mentioned in the original Book of Mormon records, but is a modern day designation for the people who came with Mulek. The Book of Mormon refers to them as the "people of Zarahemla." (Omni 1:14-16)

*   *   *

INSIGHT # FOUR: THE BOOK OF MORMON DOES NOT USE SIR NAMES AND CERTAIN FIRST NAMES ARE USED OVER AND OVER FOR SEVERAL DIFFERENT INDIVIDUALS. Many popular names in the Book of Mormon are used again and again, just as we do today, naming sons after fathers, or a child after a person that we admire. How many Johns, Jasons, and Jennifers do you know? In the Book of Mormon, there are four great men named Nephi, four-named Lehi, two Mosiahs, two Almas, two Ammons, four Jacobs, and at least two great men named Moroni. They did not use nomenclature such as Alma Senior and Alma Junior, nor any sir names. Therefore throughout this book, these people will be referred to as Nephi the 1st, Nephi the 2nd, Alma the 1st, Alma the 2nd and so on, as it relates to their Book of Mormon index designation, Nephi1, Nephi2, Alma1, Alma2, etc. This will make referencing them a little easier, as well as keeping who's who straight in the context of the book, and hopefully make things a little less confusing.

11

* * *

INSIGHT # FIVE: THE DESIGNATIONS JEW, NEPHITE, AND LAMANITE DO NOT HAVE THE SAME MEANING IN EVERY CONTEXT.

In the most restricted sense, Jew refers to the direct blood descendants of Judah. Judah was the original patriarch of the tribe of Judah, and just one of the sons of father Jacob who had eleven other sons, each of them being the head of a specific tribe in the house of Israel.

However, in its most common usage, Jew refers to all the people remaining in the Jerusalem after the Ten Tribes departed, leaving behind the so called Kingdom of Judah consisting mainly of the tribes of Judah and Benjamin, but in addition, some scattered remnants of the other tribes of Israel that were also left behind in Jerusalem at the time of the great division of Israel.

Although it is technically inaccurate, the word Jew is often used in a considerably more general sense such as any member of the House of Israel anywhere in the world. Nephi said he had charity for the Jew; "I mean them from whence I came", even though he, himself, and his family were literal descendants of the tribe of Joseph now residing on the other side of the world.

Sometimes, the word Jew is used to refer to the collective House of Israel, including adopted members of any race, creed, or color, such as it is used in the title page of the Book of Mormon in the phrase "the convincing of the Jew and Gentile that Jesus is the Christ" which divides the people of the entire world into only two camps.

A similar complexity occurs with the Nephites and the Lamanites. In the beginning, those names referred to blood descendants of Nephi and his group of righteous followers, and the same for Laman and Lemuel and their unrighteous followers. After hundreds of years of the cycles of war and peace, and the interaction of a variety of Book of Mormon peoples, the names Nephites and Lamanites became more generalized and meant only a designation between the two opposing factions. Sometimes, these opposing factions during certain periods consisted of righteous Lamanites living among the Nephites, as well as the apostate Nephites living with the Lamanites, and many other complicated social situations in the different societies.

At one point, after the appearance and resurrection of Jesus Christ in the Western Hemisphere, the people were united into only one group of righteous people, and there were no "ites" of any kind for nearly two hundred years. But then wickedness and contention slowly crept back in among the people and they divided once again into their two warring factions.

In general though, the people who kept the sacred records even though they were sometimes wicked were the Nephites, and the people who continually sought to destroy the people who kept the sacred records were the Lamanites.

By the way, the Nephites were not always the good guys, even though they had the sacred records, the Lord's prophets, and abundant opportunities to repent and stay on the straight and narrow, they would eventually become even more wicked than the Lamanites.

*   *   *

INSIGHT # SIX: THE BOOK OF MORMON DOES NOT GIVE US ENOUGH DETAILED GEOGRAPHICAL INFORMATION TO DIRECTLY RELATE BOOK OF MORMON LANDS TO TODAY'S GEOGRAPHY. Therefore the LDS church does not have an official position on exactly how Book of Mormon geography coincides with today's map of the Western hemisphere. Scholars and amateur geographers have come up with over sixty possible maps and locations. In the early days of the church, it was commonly thought that the Book of Mormon lands encompassed all of North and South America, while today many members of the church are sure that the entirety of the Book of Mormon events took place in North America only.

However, most scholars believe that the chief geographical reference in the Book of Mormon, which is the "narrow neck of land", is either the Isthmus of Panama in Central America or the Isthmus of Tehuantepec in the southern area of Mexico. This idea is possibly supported by ancient temples and other archeological sites in Central America, as well as that area being prone to volcanoes and earthquakes that were alluded to in 3rd Nephi during the great destruction of the land just before the appearance of Christ in this hemisphere.

*   *   *

(Encyclopedia of Mormonism: "John L. Sorenson (b. 1924) examines the text of the Book of Mormon. He carefully analyzes the Mesoamerican evidence, particularly the geography, climatic conditions, modes of life and warfare, and archaeological remains in An Ancient American Setting for the Book of Mormon, in order to create a plausible, coherent matrix for understanding the book. With regard to Book of Mormon geography, Sorenson concludes that the events recorded in the Book of Mormon occurred in a fairly restricted area of southern Mexico and Guatemala: He says; "The narrow neck of land is the Isthmus of Tehuantepec. The east sea is the Gulf of Mexico or its component, the Gulf of Campeche. The west sea is the Pacific Ocean to the west of Mexico and Guatemala. The land southward comprises that portion of Mexico east and south of the Isthmus of Tehuantepec . . . . The land northward consists of part of Mexico west and north of the Isthmus of Tehuantepec . . . . The final battleground where both Jaredite and Nephite peoples met their end was around the Tuxtla Mountains of south-central Veracruz" [pp. 46-47]. Encyclopedia of Mormonism, Vol.1, BOOK OF MORMON STUDIES

* * *

John A. Widtsoe, an apostle, said, "All such studies are legitimate, but the conclusions drawn from them, though they may be correct, must at the best be held as intelligent conjectures" (Vol. 3, p. 93 Widtsoe, John A. Evidences and Reconciliations, 3 vols. Salt Lake City, 1951)

President Joseph F. Smith pretty well summarized the official position of the church regarding Book of Mormon geography and the correlation with modern day geographical maps. He simply said the "Lord has not yet revealed it." Although this may leave some of us Book of Mormon "geography nuts" somewhat frustrated, we are nonetheless resigned to accept it for the time being. Although no definite correlation can be made with modern geography, the internal geography of the Book of Mormon remains remarkably consistent, refuting the idea that it was all contrived by the imagination of Joseph Smith.

In conclusion, there are two main geographical references in the Book of Mormon. They are mentioned in the books of Alma and in Ether. Wherever they may be at, Alma 22:27 talks about the "narrow strip of wilderness" and then in verse 32, it speaks of the "small neck of land." Ether 10:20 calls it "the narrow neck of land." These two chief geographical references will be our primary reference points to keep us straight in the Book of Mormon lands.

One other note on Book of Mormon geography should be mentioned. In our society, when a person says they went down to a certain place, we automatically think that they traveled south. In the opposite vein, when we use a phrase like "I'm driving up to Montana", it means we'll be traveling north. Up and down were not compass directions for the Nephites. This was not understood nor used in their culture. When the Nephites said they went down to Zarahemla from the land of Nephi, they meant they were going to a place of lower elevation, but the direction was actually north to Zarahemla, not south. We know this from clues such as the river Sidon in the Land of Nephi flowing downward from its elevated headwaters in the south wilderness to the land of Zarahemla in the north. We can conclude that Zarahemla was definitely north of the "land of original inheritance" where Father Lehi and his family had originally landed, as well as being north of the land of Nephi, as we can reasonably infer from Alma 22:27-33.

The last chapter of Alma contains another very interesting entry related to geography. It speaks of a large number of people leaving Zarahemla "into the land northward." They were led north by a man named Hagoth who took them to the borders of Bountiful "by the land Desolation." There at the west sea by the "narrow neck which led into the land northward" they built a large ship and sailed to an unknown land. From these scriptures we can deduce that the great Nephite city of Zarahemla was situated in the middle lands, with the land of Lehi-Nephi lying to the south, while the narrow neck of land, the land of Bountiful, and the land of Desolation, all lay to the north of Zarahemla. (Alma 63:4-5)

16

Although trying to reconcile Book of Mormon geography with a modern day map may leave us frustrated and completely unsatisfied, we must remember that the real value of the Book of Mormon lies not in its geography or in the attempted mapping of an ancient world, but in a far greater purpose, that being its overall spiritual message, its great wisdom, and the most profound warnings that can be given to a people. "Therefore, wo be unto the Gentiles if it so be that they harden their hearts against the Lamb of God." 1 Nephi 14:6

* * *

CHAPTER TWO

* * *

RECORDS OF THE JAREDITES

Book of Mormon history really starts thousands of years ago in the ancient Middle East, possibly somewhere in the vicinity of today's southern Iraq. This was at the time of the Great Tower and after the Great flood of Noah's time. (see Genesis 11:1-9)

"According to the Book of Mormon, the Jaredites began their migration to this land at the time when the great tower of Babel was under construction. This occurred in about the year 2200 B.C. At this time the language of the people was confused. This tower has been identified in our modern time at a place called Hillah in modern Iraq, southwest of the city of Baghdad, on the east bank of the Euphrates River". (President Alvin R. Dyer, Gen. Conference Oct. 1968)

* * *

After the Lord confused the languages of the wicked, a righteous man, named Jared and his brother commonly called "The Brother of Jared", prayed to have their family's language not confused. The Lord not only answered their prayers by not confusing their language but also directed them to a promised land. Under the direction of the

Lord, the Brother of Jared and his people built eight submarine-like barges lighted by 16 stones touched by the finger of the Lord, and made their way across the great waters to the Americas, "into a land which is choice above all the lands of the Earth." (See B of M—Ether: chapters 1 & 2 & 6)

They multiplied and became a great civilization north of "the narrow neck" of land, later to be called "the land of Desolation" by the Nephites because it was "covered with bones of men, and of beasts, and was also covered with ruins of buildings of every kind . . ." How it became a land of desolation is a long history of wars and great violence between righteous and wicked kings, between law abiding people and the secret combinations. Finally the people in general were corrupted by the desire for power, the greed for riches, deplorable whoredoms, and a disrespect and ignorance of the importance of what their prophets were telling them. After hundreds and hundreds of years of very cruel war, they finally destroyed their own civilization down to the last man, which was the last ruler of the Jaredites, Coriantumr the 2nd. Coriantumr the 1st was one of the sons of a Jaredite King named Omer, who fought his own brother to restore his father's kingdom, but was not particularly prominent in Jaredite history.

On the other hand, Coriantumr the 2nd was an important figure who was the last of the Jaredite kings. After the great and final civil war ending with the complete annihilation of the Jaredite people, there remained only two men to fight in that very last battle. As the fight came to its conclusion, there was a long bout of hand-to-hand combat that ended with King Coriantumr the 2nd finally besting Shiz, a wicked man who was the last leader of the totally evil Jaredite secret combinations. At that point, Coriantumr "smote off" the head of Shiz bringing to pass the final act of the complete and total destruction of the Jaredite civilization.

19

Though wounded himself, King Coriantumr wandered the land aimlessly. He was finally discovered by the people of Mulek who lived in the city of Zarahemla and "he dwelt with them for the space of nine moons." Later, when the righteous Nephites under the leadership of Mosiah the 1st, discovered the people of Mulek at Zarahemla, the Mulekites as they are sometimes called, showed King Mosiah a large stone engraved with the story of this King Coriantumr and all his people. King Mosiah by the power of God was able to translate the engraved stone with its sad account of the final days of the Jaredites.

Several years and three generations later, a more detailed history came forth. Called the 24 gold plates of the Jaredites, it was the historical writings of the last Jaredite prophet, who was the prophet Ether. He not only recorded his own genealogy and Jaredite history all the way back to Jared and the Great Tower, but outlined Biblical history from the beginning starting with the creation of Adam continuing down to the time of the Great Tower. These plates were discovered in "the land of desolation" north of "the narrow neck" of land by an unsuccessful expedition to find Zarahemla by the people of King Limhi, a Nephite King in the land of Nephi. After King Limhi's Nephite people were united with Mosiah's Nephite people in Zarahemla, he turned the 24 gold plates over to King Mosiah the 2nd in Zarahemla for translation and safekeeping.

Finally, hundreds of years later, the man who would become the last of the Book of Mormon writers, known as Moroni the 2nd, abridged the Jaredite history on the gold plates. He recorded his translation in the Book of Ether towards the end of the Book of Mormon period. Then after 1400 years of being hidden in the earth, these same sacred records were revealed to the Prophet Joseph Smith and he then, by the power of God, translated them for us so that we can now read all about the Jaredites in the Book of Ether as we find this fascinating history neatly tucked away in the pages of the Book of Mormon.

The Book of Ether recounts the tales of a great civilization, the story of the Jaredite people who lived, fought, and died somewhere north of "the narrow neck" of land. In the end, they left only their bleached bones and the broken down ruins of a destroyed civilization as their legacy, all because they ignored and stubbornly refused to heed the warnings of their prophets and the commandments of the Lord.

*   *   *

CHAPTER THREE

*   *   *

FATHER LEHI

Lehi's lineage, as well as the entire history of the Jews and the House of Israel, basically began nearly 4000 years ago in the ancient Middle East with Father Abraham in the ancient city of Ur of Chaldees. This city-state of the great Sumerian civilization is thought to have been located somewhere in today's southern Iraq near the confluence of the Tigris and Euphrates rivers. Religious persecution by idol worshipers sent Abraham and his family on a long journey north up the Euphrates River to Haran on the southern border of modern Turkey where the fertile plateaus were good for grazing. After living there several years and then making covenants with the Lord there, Abraham was sent by the Lord, along with his family, down to the South Eastern end of the Mediterranean to the legendary "Promised Land" known today as Israel.

This was the land of Canaan in Abraham's time, but today it is called Palestine, or the Holy Land. The country of Israel has occupied most of the Holy Land since 1947, and it is still disputed real estate after thousands of years of contentious claims. Many centuries ago as the Children of Israel entered Canaan, they battled with the ancient Canaanites, and then after that, they had were further conflicts and came under the repressive rule of the Babylonians, the Persians, the Macedonians, Rome, the Byzantine Empire, Muslim Arabs, and the Muslim Ottomans. The conflicts continue to this day in the Holy Land with regular eruptions of violence and the continuing caustic political disputes between modern day Jews and the Muslim Palestinians. In fact, there is animosity towards Israel from most of the Muslim Arab world and the constantly irascible Iranians, who technically should have no land disputes with Israel.

The scriptures indicate that all of these afflictions have come upon Israel because of their past disobedience to God, their worship of idols, and the crucifixion of their own Messiah. The Holy land seems to have been destined to never be at rest until Israel accepts Jesus Christ as the Messiah and then He himself will bring peace to that land. For further reading, see (Genesis chap. 11 to 25, Pearl of Great Price—Abraham 1 & 2)

Abraham received the Abrahamic covenant from the Lord, which in part included a promise of having posterity like the sands of the sea, like the stars of the sky. That promise was fulfilled through three principal lines of Abrahamic descendents, coming by way of his sons, Ishmael, Isaac, and a third line through his sons descended through his third wife Keturah.

This all came about due to his first wife Sarah being barren. She therefore, under an unwritten law of tradition, fulfilled her wifely obligation to give her husband a son to carry on his name by giving her handmaiden, Hagar the Egyptian, to Abraham for wife. That union produced a son, Ishmael, who became the father of twelve princes, and the legendary patriarch of the royal ancestors of the nomadic Arab tribes of the Arabian Peninsula.

At the ripe old age of one hundred, Abraham and his wife Sarah begat his second son Isaac, who being the true son of promise would then receive the Abrahamic covenant and blessings. Unfortunately, this has become an ongoing point of argument by the Muslim world, which claims that Ishmael, being Abraham's eldest son, was actually the one who received the covenant and blessings and that those blessing included the inheritance of the Promised Land now known as Palestine. Neither the Israelis nor the Palestinians will compromise on this point nor give up their long-standing traditional and historical claims.

Abraham's son, Isaac, with his wife Rebekah, begat Abraham's twin grandsons, Esau and Jacob. Even though Jacob was the younger son, his mother was inspired to know that he would be the next one to receive the Abrahamic covenant. Owing to a family squabble over the birthright, the exiled Jacob went to live with his mother's brother, his uncle Laban, who had two daughters, Leah and Rachel. Jacob only desired to have Rachel, but ended up with four wives, which bore him 12 sons and a daughter. One of his twelve sons was young Joseph, the future ancestor of Father Lehi. After being sold as a slave into Egypt, he found favor with the Pharaoh and eventually became an Egyptian ruler saving Egypt from famine. When the famine also hit Canaan, this gave Joseph an opportunity to manipulate his own brothers and his father Jacob into bringing the rest of the family into Egypt to save them from the famine. There in Egypt, their family would evolve into the twelve tribes of the House of Israel and become the great nation of the Hebrews under the rule of the Egyptians.

Four hundred years later, the chosen one, Moses would deliver them from years of bondage and eventually lead them back to the Land of Canaan, the perpetual Promised Land. With their large numbers and under a system of judges beginning with Joshua, who was Moses' designated successor, they became a strong, powerful, and a war like people, battling often with their neighbors who considered them to be aggressive intruders. After two hundred years of rule by the judges of Israel, including such interesting ones as the legendary Samson, and Deborah the militant lady judge, the Elders of Israel insisted on a king to rule over them. The last judge of Israel who was called Samuel the Prophet, was then inspired by the Lord to anoint the young Saul as the first King of Israel. (1 Samuel 8:4-7, 9:15-17)

Under the succession of the three great Kings of Israel, Saul, David, and Solomon, the country of Israel would prosper greatly, become a wealthy nation, and reach the zenith of Israel's power and geographical extent and become a strong economic and military force to be dealt with in the land of Canaan.

After King Solomon died, ending his great and powerful reign, ten of the tribes rebelled against his much less wiser son, Rehoboam, and then left to form the Northern Kingdom of Israel under the misguided leadership of an Ephraimite, called Jeroboam. Unfortunately and in-spite of repeated warnings by their prophets, including the great prophets Elijah, Hosea, and Amos, they drifted into idol worship and became ripe for destruction. In about 722 B.C. the Assyrians accommodated them, took them into captivity and the "Ten Lost Tribes" would lose their freedom, their culture, their identity, and consequently, if not infamously, become lost to the world and to history. See (1Kings chap. 11 & 12, 2 Kings chap 17)

The Southern Kingdom of Judah based in Jerusalem, consisting mainly of the tribes of Judah and Benjamin, complemented with a smattering of most of the other tribes, would also ignore the warnings of their prophets, most particularly the prophets Isaiah, Jeremiah, and Ezekiel. While the so-called "Jews" came to disrespect and ignore their own living God, they gradually became worshipers of false Gods and idols in high places and even stoned their own prophets.

Justifiably Jerusalem too, would be destroyed, and the Babylonian army under King Nebuchadnezzar would raze the city, round up the inhabitants, and take the "Jews" into captivity in about 587 B.C., where they would remain in bondage for the next fifty years.

A few years before the prophesied destruction of Jerusalem and captivity of the Jews, the Lord came in a vision to a righteous man living in Jerusalem by the name of Lehi. This was in about 600 B.C.; or about thirteen years before the fall of Jerusalem, at which time the Lord chose to preserve Father Lehi and his family. They were technically not Jews, but descendants of Joseph who was sold in to Egypt, the same Joseph who was the seed of Jacob, who's seed would become the remnant of the House of Israel that the Lord would preserve through Father Lehi and his sons. (1Nephi 5:14-16, 2Nephi 3:5)

While Father Lehi was living in Jerusalem during the first year of the reign of King Zedekiah, he prayed with all of his heart to the Lord, and a pillar of fire appeared before him and he heard a voice. In this vision and another in his own house, Lehi saw the Savior Jesus Christ, the twelve apostles, and the destruction and captivity of Jerusalem. His obligations were clear. (1 Nephi: 1)

Though his only motive was to warn and save the people of Jerusalem from the coming destruction, they mocked him and even sought his life. Subsequently, in an inspired dream, the Lord then commanded Lehi to take his family and the Plates of Brass, which were the records of Jews, and go in to the wilderness to be saved from certain destruction.

The wicked Laban, a distant relative of Father Lehi through their ancestors, was also a descendant of Joseph who was sold into Egypt. He just happened to have the ancestral family history of the Jews in his possession. These valuable records, written on the Plates of Brass, were legally his, but unfortunately he being a very wicked man, would not be the one to put them to good use and was less than cooperative in turning the records over to Lehi's sons even after they had offered him their family's valuables. He not only took their gold and silver by force but also ordered his servants to slay them. After Laman, Lemuel, Sam, and Nephi had barely escaped with their lives and had failed to get the plates, the three oldest brothers were ready to give up having no doubt in their minds that they had done all that they could do. But Lehi's obedient and faithful young son, Nephi, insisted that the Lord "giveth no commandments" unless He would provide a way for the commandment to be obeyed. Thus being inspired by the spirit of the Lord; "it is better that one man should perish than that a nation should dwindle and perish in unbelief", he was constrained to assassinate Laban and retrieve the records. (1 Nephi 4:13)

The importance of this deed was later proven out in the case of the people of Mulek who took no records with them and so did "dwindle in unbelief" and lost their religious heritage, their own original language, and even their belief in God.

Then with Laban's servant Zoram in tow and the plates of Brass under his arm, Nephi with his brothers returned to the camp of Father Lehi in the wilderness to the great joy of their worried mother. Soon after their return, the Lord spoke to Father Lehi again saying "..it was not meet for him, Lehi, that he should take his family into the wilderness alone; but that his sons should take daughters to wife.." So once again Nephi and his brothers returned to Jerusalem, this time to go to the house of Ishmael, who had two sons and five daughters. "The Lord did soften the heart of Ishmael" who was touched by the spirit of the Lord and amazingly agreed to leave his home and all of his possessions behind, and take his wife and children and follow Lehi's family into an unknown and dangerous wilderness. (1 Nephi 7:4-5)

While traveling in the wilderness, Father Lehi and Sariah bore two more sons, Jacob and Joseph. Nephi also had sisters, but their names and the account of their births are not given. (2 Nephi 5:6)

During this time, Father Lehi also received his vision of "the tree of life." Nephi having a righteous desire to know the meaning of the vision, was caught up by the spirit, taken to a high mountain and shown the meaning of "the tree of life." He was also shown a vision of the birth, ministry, and crucifixion of the Savior, as well as the ministry of the Twelve Apostles. The rise and fall of Nephi's own people in the Promised Land was shown to him, not to mention the loathsome and filthy state of his surviving brethren, the Lamanites. He saw Columbus sailing to America to the seed of his brethren, the Lamanites, and the beginning of their foretold scattering by the gentiles. He saw the Pilgrims coming to America, the Revolutionary war with Great Britain, the independence and prosperity of America, and the Bible being carried upon the face of the land even though many "plain and precious parts" were taken from it by the great and abominable church. He saw the coming forth of the Book of Mormon and it being carried forth to his Lamanite brethren by the Gentiles, and many more things that he was not allowed to write. See (1Nephi: chapters 11,12, &13)

After eight years of sore trials and arduous travel, while guided by the Liahona, which was a unique compass made of brass which they called a "round ball of curious workmanship", the Lehi party finally arrived at the seashore on the south east coast of the Arabian Peninsula in the Persian Gulf. We deduce this from Nephi's uncannily accurate description of their travels combined with modern sleuthing and satellite imagery and mapping.

(see http://www.jefflindsay.com/BMEvidences.shtml)

They called the sea at this point, "Irreantum" wherein 1st Nephi 17:5 declares the meaning to be "many waters." This word along with the word Liahona causes some critics of the Book of Mormon to laugh at the concocted words of Joseph Smith. A non-LDS author, Rabbi Yoseph ben Yehuda explains that in the ancient Egyptian language, "Ir" means river, "re" means mouth, "na" translates to many and "tehem" to water. So Irreantum then "sounds like a great name to give to the ocean while standing in a wadi where a large fresh water lagoon and a seasonal river meets the sea."—Rabbi Yoseph

Rabbi Yoseph also explains the word Lihona, the name by which Lehi's unusual compass was called, saying that it contains perfectly good root words in Hebrew that apply appropriately to the purpose and use of the Liahona. Once again, Joseph Smith's supposed fantasy story contains very unusual words with actual Middle Eastern roots that an uneducated New York farm boy would be highly unlikely to have known, nor that any of his associates would have known. (see www.JeffLindsay.com/LDSFAQ/ or (www.jefflindsay/BMevidences.shtml)

*   *   *

The primitive seaside port where Lehi's family rested, was amazingly well supplied with every thing they needed to replenish body and spirit, as well as materials for building a ship. They called the place Bountiful. There, Nephi was commanded to build a ship to transport the family to the Promised Land across the sea. Laman and Lemuel responded in their usual way. "Our brother is a fool for he thinketh that he can build a ship; yea, and he also thinketh that he can

Shell Abegglen

cross these great waters." Despite the brazen threats, the harassment, and the loudly expressed doubts of Laman and Lemuel, Nephi under the direction of the Lord, was able to build a seaworthy ship, in which "the workmanship was exceedingly fine" and they embarked upon a long journey. After sailing for the space of many days upon the open waters, which was possibly two years (591-589 B.C.), and nearly being swallowed up by the sea, they finally arrived in the Americas, "The Promised Land." (1 Nephi Chapters 17 & 18)

They pitched their tents, tilled the earth, planted seeds of all kinds that they had brought from Jerusalem, and they were blessed in abundance. They also discovered all kinds of animal life, as well as "all manner of ore." As commanded by the Lord, Nephi took some of the ore, made metal plates and began his record keeping in "the learning of the Jews and the language of the Egyptians." (1 Nephi 1:2) He also abridged the writings of his father's dreams, visions, and prophesies. (1 Nephi 19:1)

Less anyone should think that the Lord is not in control of his Kingdom even 2400 years into the future, Nephi's personal and inspired abridgement of "The Book of Lehi" which was his own father's writings, would save the day a couple of thousand years later when Joseph Smith's scribe, Martin Harris, would unintentionally lose Father Lehi's writings. Thus the more important aspects of Lehi's records were preserved and most significantly there was nothing vital lost from our scriptures.

Father Lehi eventually waxing old and becoming even more prophetic, prophesied many things concerning his seed. He also repeated the prophecies of Joseph who was sold in to Egypt, concerning a latter day prophet whose name would also be Joseph and would bring forth the Book of Mormon to "cry from the dust" for the repentance of Joseph's posterity.

". . . For Joseph truly testified, saying: A seer shall the Lord my God raise up, who shall be a choice seer unto the fruit of my loins . . . And his name shall be called after me; and it shall be after the name of his father . . ." (Joseph Smith's father was Joseph Smith Senior)

"And the words which he shall write shall be the words which are expedient in my wisdom should go forth unto the fruit of thy loins . . . . And they shall cry from the dust; yea, even repentance unto their brethren . . ." (2 Nephi 3:5-22)

The prophesies of Joseph who was sold into Egypt, as well as the Book of Joseph are not in the Old Testament, and though Joseph Smith indicated that he had acquired them at the time that he received the record of Abraham, apparently he was not allowed to publish the writings of Joseph at that particular period of time. Therefore, we must be content with Lehi's brief description of the prophesies of Joseph concerning a choice seer called Joseph.

*   *   *

(Oliver Cowdery remembered that it was "two rolls . . . [with] two or three other small pieces," the text written "with black, and a small part, red ink or paint" (Messenger and Advocate, Dec. 31, 1835). Within three days, Joseph Smith translated some "hieroglyphics, and much to our joy found that one of the rolls contained the writings of Abraham, another, writings of Joseph of Egypt."—Encyclopedia of Mormonism, Vol.3, PAPYRI, JOSEPH SMITH:)

*   *   *

As mentioned earlier, Father Lehi, had kept his own account of his family's travels in the wilderness in what was the Book of

Lehi, but that too was not to be published due to the Martin Harris incident, resulting in the loss of the first 116 pages of the Book of Mormon manuscript. This event would become a significant lesson in obedience, both to Brother Harris and the prophet Joseph Smith. (see D&C Sec. 3 heading & verses 1-14)

Father Lehi told his sons that he knew that Jerusalem had been destroyed because of a vision, which he had been shown, and he knew with certainty that if they had remained there, they too would have been destroyed. He also reminded Laman and Lemuel just how blessed they had been by the Lord, and even though they had suffered many afflictions, they were even now being blessed by being in a promised land, and he chastised them for their periodic rebellion. He also spoke to Laman and Lemuel's sons and daughters and blessed them. He counseled his younger sons, Jacob and Joseph at length, and reminded them to hearken to the words of their brother Nephi. He told his older son, Sam, that his family would be blessed along with Nephi's. Then after counseling his entire household by the spirit of the Lord, including Zoram the servant of Laban, he blessed all his sons and their posterity. Father Lehi then passed away and was buried. (2 Nephi chapter 4)

Not many days later, Laman and Lemuel became completely intolerable as they criticized their younger brother Nephi for trying to preach to them against their wishes. The way they saw it, their younger brother was trying to be a ruler over them, even though they were the eldest and they should rightfully be the ones to rule over him. Their anger festered and grew to the point that they did seek the life of Nephi and actually plotted to slay him.

The Lord then spoke to Nephi, ". . . Inasmuch as they will not hearken unto thy words they shall be cut off from the presence of the Lord. And behold they were cut off from his presence." (2 Nephi 5:20)

Warned by the Lord to separate from his hostile older brothers, Nephi the 1st took his family and all those who would follow after him, left the land of Lehi, "the land of original inheritance," and fled into the wilderness with little more than a prayer, a lot of faith, and a new hope for living in peace somewhere far from their tormentors, as they continued to try to be obedient to the commandments of the Lord. (2 Nephi chapter 5)

*   *   *

CHAPTER FOUR

*   *   *

SCHISM

Traveling "for the space of many days", Nephi took his family, his elder brother Sam, his younger brothers Jacob and Joseph, his sisters, and Zoram the servant of Laban, and all of their families with him into the wilderness. They also carried with them the plates of brass, the "ball or compass", and the sword of Laban. When they felt safe from the evilness of their older brothers, they pitched their tents and established a suitable place as their new home, a place still way south of "the narrow neck of land" and also still south of what would be called the "narrow strip of wilderness." They called their new home the land of Nephi. Eventually, the entire area south of the "narrow strip of wilderness" would be called the land of Lehi-Nephi.

The people of Nephi then did prosper exceedingly, sewing and reaping, raising flocks and herds, and multiplying in the land and becoming a great people. They also copied the sword of Laban making many weapons to defend themselves against the hatred of Laman and Lemuel's followers.

The schism between Nephi the 1st and his elder brothers would evolve into a thousand years of war and a perpetual feud between the two major peoples of the Book of Mormon, the Nephites and the Lamanites. Because of their iniquity, the Lord did cause a skin of darkness to come on the Lamanites, so that they would not be enticing to the Nephites. (2 Nephi 5:21)

Unfortunately, the Nephite generations following the early Nephites were not always the good guys, even though they had plenty of prophets to lead them and the words of the sacred records to keep them on the straight and narrow.

Meanwhile, Nephi did build a temple after the manner of the Temple of Solomon, though not quite as elaborate, but still of exceedingly fine workmanship. Under the direction of the Lord, he began keeping two records. The small plates were for spiritual matters and the large plates would chronicle the reign of the Nephite kings in a more secular history.

He also consecrated his younger brothers, Jacob and Joseph, to be priest and teachers. Nephi and his brothers taught the people of Nephi many important things, including a great deal of teaching from the Old Testament writings of the prophet Isaiah. (2 Nephi 5:26)

The general theme of Isaiah's teachings was that Israel would be scattered and cursed due to their disobedience, but that a great gentile nation would rise in the promised land, that the gentiles would bring the gospel to Israel so that they would recognize their true Savior, and that Israel would be gathered to the lands of their inheritance fulfilling the covenant of Abraham. Apparently, and probably being inspired to do so, Nephi felt that some of the writings of Isaiah were so important to future readers that they needed to be included in his own records nearly word for word. (See 1 Nephi chap. 22) (Isaiah chapters 2-14)

Nephi being inspired by the spirit also spoke many words directly from Jesus Christ concerning the last days, warning against the many false churches and false teachers who would teach much false doctrine.

In 2 Nephi 29:10, Christ says very pointedly "Wherefore, because that ye have a Bible ye need not suppose that it contains all my words; neither need ye suppose that I have not caused more to be written."

2 Nephi 29:11, "For I command all men, both in the east and in the west, and in the north, and in the south, and in the islands of the sea, that they shall write the words which I speak unto them . . ."

These hallowed words in the scriptures from Jesus Christ, once again validate the purpose, the authenticity, the truth, and the authority of Book of Mormon's very existence, negating all the skepticism, mockery, and unfounded spiteful accusations of its many critics.

Nephi the 1st was a very strong person, physically, mentally, and spiritually. His steadfast obedience to the Lord was unparalleled and he was a hero for all ages and times, even for future generations and the Centuries to come. The people of Nephi loved him dearly and even wanted him to be their King, for he had worked hard for the majority of the days of his life for their welfare, and he had skillfully wielded the sword of Laban as he risked his life in the defense of his people. Although he did wisely decline to be their King, before his death, he anointed a choice leader to be King and protector over them. In honor of their beloved Nephi, the people then called their new King, Second Nephi, and their succeeding kings, Third Nephi, Fourth Nephi and so on.

These Nephite Kings who succeeded Nephi the 1st should not to be confused with the future great prophets with very similar titles who were the descendants of the great prophet Alma, his famed missionary son Alma the 2nd, and his courageous grandson, commander Helaman. These very important descendants of Alma would in the future become the prophets Nephi the 2nd, Nephi the 3rd, and Nephi the 4th, and become special servants of the Lord, as well as significant Book of Mormon authors and sacred record keepers. (Jacob 1:9-11)

*   *   *

CHAPTER FIVE

* * *

JACOB—BROTHER OF NEPHI AND HIS DESCENDANTS

Jacob, the younger brother of Nephi the 1st, continued Nephi's legacy of being a sacred record keeper and also being a very strong spiritual leader to his people. Because Jacob had been brought up during the trials and tribulations of the eight-year trek in the wilderness, after his family had left their home in Jerusalem, and had endured the dangerous crossing of the great sea, and then had suffered the lost of his parents, and finally had went through the big family break up resulting in the unhappy separation from his wicked older and disobedient brothers, he sometimes felt and sounded forlorn. He wrote ". . . our lives passed away like as it were unto us a dream, we being a lonesome and a solemn people, wanderers, cast out from Jerusalem, born in tribulation, in a wilderness, and hated of our brethren, which caused wars and contentions; wherefore, we did mourn out our days." (Jacob 7:26)

He also felt a heavy burden, that if he did not do his part to teach and warn the Nephite people of the consequences of straying from the Lord's commandments, that the sin would be upon his own head. Unfortunately, by the time of the reign of the second

King of the Nephites, the people were already preoccupied with riches, polygamy and concubines. Greatly concerned about their worldliness, he taught them that, "But before you seek for riches, seek ye for the kingdom of God. And after ye have obtained a hope in Christ ye shall obtain riches, if ye seek them; and ye will seek them for the intent to do good-to clothe the naked, and to feed the hungry . . ." (Jacob 2:18-19) Jacob was even more bold and plainspoken as he warned against pride, polygamy and concubines, saying that they were an abomination before the Lord. Emphasizing the lord's position, he quoted "For I, the Lord, delight in the chastity of women. And whoredoms are an abomination before me . . ." (Jacob 2:28) He chastened them further saying, "Behold ye have done greater iniquities than the Lamanites, our brethren. Ye have broken the hearts of your tender wives, and lost the confidence of your children, because of your bad example before them;" (Jacob 2:35) It was not unusual for him to express disappointment, grief, and anxiety over the waywardness of his people.

Even so, despite Jacob's discouragement, Sherem the great flatterer and anti-Christ could not shake Jacob or his testimony. Jacob said, "I truly had seen angels, and they had ministered unto me. And also, I had heard the voice of the Lord speaking unto me in very word, from time to time." (Jacob 7:5)

When the evil provoker Sherem, challenged Jacob to show him a sign "by the power of the Holy Ghost", Jacob told him that he did not wish to be tempting the Lord God to show signs; never-the-less, God's will be done. At that point, Sherem did receive a sign, a sign that he regretted asking for, a sign that did cause him to fall to the earth. Before he died, he told the multitude that he had been deceived by the power of the Devil. He denied all the evil that he had preached, then repented and testified of Christ and the truth of the scriptures, and in the end, he "gave up the ghost" and passed on to wait for his final judgment.

The multitude was astonished by Sherem's confession and testimony. The spirit of the Lord then overcame them as they fell to the earth and had their faith restored. They also were blessed with a renewed interest in diligently searching the scriptures. (Jacob 7:13-21)

Often preaching from the words of the prophet Isaiah, Jacob also quoted Zenos, another Old Testament prophet, whose words have been lost from our present Bible. Apparently the Plates of Brass contained the words of more than just the one lost prophet. In addition to Zenos, there were other lost prophets whose words were removed during the many uninspired translations of our modern Bible. (1 Nephi 19:10) Jacob quotes the prophet Zenos in Jacob chapter 5, one of the longest chapters in scripture, as he cites the famous allegory of the wild and tame olive trees. The allegory illustrates the adoption of the faithful into the House of Israel as a promise given to Abraham that through him, all nations of the earth would be blessed.

*   *   *

"All of these promises were made to Abraham because of his faithfulness. No person who is not of Israel can become a member of the Church without becoming of the house of Israel by adoption . . . . This doctrine of adoption, or grafting in of the wild olive branches into the tame olive tree, was understood by the prophets of Israel. It was taught by John the Baptist and by the Savior and is expressed most emphatically and beautifully in the parable of the tame olive tree in the 5th chapter of Jacob, in the Book of Mormon." Joseph Fielding Smith Jr., Doctrines of Salvation, Vol.3, p.247

*   *   *

"The allegory of the olive tree in Jacob 5 shows a clear knowledge of olive cultivation far beyond what Joseph Smith, growing up in the American Northeast, could have possessed. But it is entirely consistent, in impressive detail, with what we learn from ancient manuals on olive cultivation." (Daniel C. Peterson, "Mounting Evidence for the Book of Mormon," Ensign, Jan. 2000, 19)

*   *   *

Jacob then commented on the Lord's compassion and individual concern for his children as he explained the allegory to his people, "And how merciful is our God unto us for he remembereth the house of Israel, both roots and branches . . ." (Jacob 6:4)

The writings of Jacob show that he had deep emotional feelings, was a gifted writer, a profound prophet, a poetic preacher, a strong spiritual leader, and a most powerful witness of Jesus Christ. (See Jacob-Son of Lehi: Encyclopedia of Mormonism)

*   *   *

Before his death, Jacob reminded his son, Enos, of promises made to their beloved Nephi, which concerned the commandment to write upon and take care of the plates, and Enos made likewise promises to his father, which was to continue the writings on the small plates of Nephi and to protect and preserve these precious sacred records.

While hunting beast in the forest and praying all day long and into the night, Enos came to know God and received a strong testimony. Not only was he greatly concerned about his own people, the Nephites, he also asked God to let the records be preserved for the benefit of the Lamanites, not with standing the fact that the Lamanites had vowed to destroy the Nephites, the Nephite records, and the traditions of their Fathers. Enos prophesied and bore testimony to his people and even had some success in that the "Nephites did seek diligently to restore the Lamanites unto the true faith in God." Unfortunately, the Lamanites were eating raw meat, worshiping idols, promoting violence, and filled with much hatred, rendering them at this point, "unteachable."

Enos saw much war during his life, and even called his own people "stiff-necked" while he continually tried to "keep them in fear of the Lord." Nevertheless, with great faith he ceased not to preach the truth of Christ all the days of his life.

Enos passed the sacred records to his son, Jarom, who was also a man of God. During the time of Jarom, most of the people were obedient to the commandments as they followed the example of their righteous leaders and Kings. Because of this, they were able to prevail against the ongoing attacks of the Lamanites and they prospered greatly in the land.

Omni, a skilled Nephite warrior who was the son of Jarom, continued in the care of the records, although admitting that he was not necessarily a righteous man, saying "I of myself am a wicked man" and he confessed that he had not kept the Lord's commandments. Two hundred and eighty two years after Lehi left Jerusalem, this Omni handed the records over to his own son, Amaron. Amaron wrote little except to say that most of the wicked Nephites were destroyed 320 years after Father Lehi, by the judgment of the Lord who had warned, "Inasmuch as ye will not keep my commandments ye shall not prosper in the land." (Omni 1:6)

Amaron, the son of Omni, then turned over the records to his brother, Chemish, who wrote only that he kept and wrote upon the records because of the commandments of their father. Chemish handed down the records to his son Abinadom, another skilled Nephite warrior who admitted that he had slain many Lamanites with his own sword in defense of his people but he still continued to care for the sacred records and wrote that he knew of no revelation or prophecy except that which had already been written, and that should be sufficient.

Then finally, just before 130 B.C., this Abinadom the mighty warrior handed the sacred records down to his son Amaleki. Amaleki continued the sacred writing upon the small plates, but with much more story to tell than the previous five writers. He tells the fascinating story of Mosiah the 1st, the Nephite refugee who left the wickedness of the land of Nephi with a small group of righteous people in about 200 B.C. Led by God to Zarahemla along with his followers, Mosiah eventually became the King of Zarahemla, the great city of the "Mulekites."

This Amaleki, the last of the record keepers on the small plates, not having a son of his own, finally turned the sacred records over to the successor and son of King Mosiah the 1st, the good King Benjamin. The records on the plates were full and this then brought an end to the writings on the Small Plates of Nephi, and also an end to Jacob's legacy of handing the records down father to son, and brother to brother.

This Amaleki, who was the last record keeper on the small plates, apparently also had access to the Large Plates of Nephi, as well. We believe this assumption to be true because five hundred years later, Commander Mormon speaking of Amaleki and the Small Plates writes ". . . he took them and put them with the other plates which contained records which had been handed down by the Kings, from generation to generation until the days of King Benjamin."

We can reasonably assume that these other plates were actually the Large Plates of Nephi, which had been kept and handed down by the Nephite Kings. The large plates recorded things of a more secular and political nature, as opposed to the more religious motif of the small plates. The small plate writings were a completely separate and different type of a record from the large plates which were more or less historical writings, while the small plates were more like a family history, and certainly more spiritual in its nature. The Small Plates were written by Nephi, Jacob, Enos, and their faithful posterity. (See W of M 1:10, 1 Nephi 9:2-4, Jarom 1:14)

*   *   *

WORDS OF MORMON

The Words of Mormon, even though they were placed in the Book of Mormon immediately after the book of Omni, were actually written more than 500 years later by the great military leader and sacred record keeper, Mormon. His purpose was to connect the history on the Small Plates of Nephi, which were closed out by Amaleki the 1st in the Book of Omni in 130 B.C., to Mormon's own abridgment of the Large Plates of Nephi which he recorded in 385 A.D., a time period of five hundred and fifteen years later. Mormon makes this important connection by picking up and continuing the story of King Benjamin, who was mentioned at the end of the small plates in the book of Omni, and then tying it in with King Benjamin's story in the Words of Mormon and finally following through with it and resuming the story of King Benjamin as it is written in the book of Mosiah.

Mormon indicates that he does not know all that the Lord has in mind and that he's not certain what all the purposes are for what he is doing, but he is certain that it is from the Lord and that it is for a wise purpose, and "..he worketh in me to do according to his will." He indicates that he knows the records will be preserved because of the great words that are written upon them, and that from these words of God, his own people and their brethren will be judged at the great and last day.

Mormon then continues his own abridgment of Nephi's large plates through the books of Mosiah, Alma, Helaman, 3rd Nephi, and 4th Nephi, and then proceeds to write Mormon chapters 1 through 7. He tells us, "I cannot write the hundredth part of the things of my people" indicating the great volume of so many records.

At that point, his son Moroni the 2nd, took over and finished Mormon chapters 8 and 9, and then added the abridgment of the Jaredite record called the book of Ether, and then finally included his own writing, the Book of Moroni, to finish out the Book of Mormon, as we know it today. This may all sound somewhat complicated and perhaps even a little confusing, but it's another proof that Joseph Smith did not fabricate the Book of Mormon, but only translated the actual accounts from multiple authors written on multiple ancient records.

For a better understanding of these record sources from ancient America, see the introductory pages at the beginning of the Book of

Mormon immediately after "The Testimony of the Prophet Joseph Smith" and just before the contents page. It is called "A Brief Explanation about The Book of Mormon." This is a great tutorial on the different metal plate sources of the Book of Mormon, briefly explaining the Plates of Nephi, the Plates of Mormon, the plates of Ether, and the Plates of Brass. It becomes plain to see that the Book of Mormon is a wonderful literary and historical record and a great spiritual work compiled from many sources through the strenuous efforts and sacrifice of many inspired servants of the Lord.

*   *   *

CHAPTER SIX

*   *   *

THE MOSIAH DYNASTY

Apparently in the days before King Mosiah the 1st made his exodus from the land of Nephi at the south end of "the narrow strip of wilderness", the Nephites had become so wicked in a period of about 400 years after the death of Nephi the 1st, that the Lord felt a need for separating the few righteous Nephites among them from the corruption of all the wicked and incorrigible Nephites that still lived in the land of Nephi. In addition to this, leaving the land of Nephi had the added benefit of getting away from the persistent hatred and relentless harassment of the Lamanites in that land.

Mosiah was one of the few righteous men left in the Land of Nephi and being close to the Lord, he was thus an inspired leader. The record keeper Amaleki writes in the book of Omni that the Lord warned Mosiah the 1st to leave and flee in to the wilderness with as many of the righteous Nephites that he could persuade to go with him, "who would hearken to the voice of the Lord." We also have to assume that Mosiah and his followers brought all the sacred records with them from the land of Nephi, although only the Plates of Brass are mentioned at that time. Later, when Mosiah's son, King Benjamin, turns over the sacred records to his own son Mosiah the 2nd, the record would specifically mention the brass plates, the plates of Nephi, the ball or director, and the sword of Laban. (Mosiah chapter one)

Mosiah the 1st and his followers made their exodus from the lands of "original inheritance", or the lands of Lehi and the adjoining lands of Nephi, and they traveled north beyond the "narrow strip of wilderness" and continued even farther north in the direction of "the narrow neck of land." They were guided through the wilderness by the spirit of God to the great city of Zarahemla, a city ruled by King Zarahemla, a descendant of Prince Mulek. This city had been established by the mysterious "Mulekites", the people of Mulek who had escaped Jerusalem at the time that King Nebuchadnezzar and the Babylonian armies had captured the Jews and destroyed Jerusalem. Brought by the hand of the Lord to the Americas in haste, they brought no records with them. By the time Mosiah the 1st and his followers had discovered the "Mulekites", they had lost their original culture, their religious heritage, their belief in God, and had even corrupted their own original language beyond the understanding of Mosiah and his followers at the time Mosiah's group joined with them.

Mosiah having compassion upon them caused them to be taught in his own language, which was their original language, or the language of the Jews. That enlightenment being combined with joy of having the Plates of Brass and the history containing their own genealogy restored to them, caused them to rally and proclaim with one voice that their true desire was that Mosiah should be their new King. Thus they all united into one people, as Mosiah's followers who were the exiled righteous Nephites from the land of Lehi-Nephi, joined with the "Mulekites" in the great city of Zarahemla under the capable leadership of King Mosiah. (Omni chapter 1)

Writing in the Book of Omni, Amaleki, the last record keeper on the small plates, wrote that he was born in the days of Mosiah the 1st, and then he quickly moves on from King Mosiah's reign to the reign of Mosiah's son, King Benjamin. He tells how there was much bloodshed and war during King Benjamin's time, between the Nephites and Lamanites, these events having taken place before King Benjamin and his armies drove the Lamanites from the land. With the help of his holy men, King Benjamin was able to establish a time of peace and rest that lasted the remainder of his days.

The record keeper Amaleki also relates that there were many of the people at this point in time, who decided that they wanted to go back down to the land of original inheritance, which was called the land of Lehi-Nephi. It turned out to be a bad idea, as many of them lost their lives, mainly because they "were slow to remember the Lord." Amaleki never did find out what happened to his own brother who went with them. Being inspired by the righteousness of King Benjamin, and having no son of his own, the record keeper Amaleki finally turns the sacred records over to King Benjamin in approximately 130 B.C., closing out the small plates of Nephi, and bringing an end to Amaleki's writings and his own days upon the Earth.

Mormon then, in 385 A.D. over 500 years later, now picks up the story of King Benjamin in the Words of Mormon and continues it in the Book of Mosiah with Mormon's own abridgment of the Large Plates of Nephi. He tells how Benjamin taught his three sons well in the language of his fathers and all about their own heritage and the importance of keeping the sacred records. The King then turns over the sacred records, the sword of Laban, and the ball or director to his son, Mosiah the 2nd.

As he began to wax old, King Benjamin commanded his son Mosiah the 2nd to make a proclamation through out the land that all the people with their individual families should gather around the temple in their tents with the tent doors facing towards the temple. When the people were ready, King Benjamin spoke many words to his people from a tall tower. The multitudes were so large that he also caused his words to be written and sent out to those who were unable to hear him directly. Then out of his own mouth, he proclaimed his son, Mosiah the 2nd, to be the new king over Zarahemla as he addressed his people for the final time.

He then expounded upon the future Advent of Christ, his ministry and his ultimate sacrifice and atonement, and he emphasized that Salvation can only come through Christ's name. The King Benjamin address goes down in scriptural history as one of the great speeches of all time as he gave his people wise council in gratitude, faith, the atonement, obedience, giving to the poor, and the call to serve each other with his famous words, "..when ye are in the service of your fellow beings ye are only in the service of your God." He also made it quite clear that even if we serve God our whole lives, we would still be unprofitable servants because he has given us so much.

When King Benjamin had finished his speech, he inquired of the people if they believed all his words. They cried with one voice that they did, that they had had a mighty change in their hearts because of his words, that they had received the spirit of the Lord, and that they were now willing to make a covenant because of it. King Benjamin therefore thought it wise to record all the names of those who did enter into the covenant to obey the Lord's commandments and "there was not one soul", except the children, who did not enter into the covenant.

King Benjamin was not only a righteous ruler, and very good to his people serving them the best way he knew how, but he imparted much wisdom for their personal benefit, and also for any who would read his many great words of wisdom centuries later. (See Mosiah chapters 2-5)

* * *

"King Benjamin's classic address in **Mosiah 2-5** occupies roughly 11 pages in the current English edition, which means that Joseph Smith may have dictated this doctrinally rich text of nearly 5,000 words in a little more than one day. Recent research shows that the sermon is intimately linked with the ancient Israelite Feast of Tabernacles and the Day of Atonement, as well as with archaic treaty and covenant formulas and early Near Eastern coronation festivals. Even the physical setting of the speech—delivered while the king stood upon a tower (see **Mosiah 2:7**)—is ritually appropriate to the occasion. But the Prophet Joseph Smith could not have learned this from the English Bibles or any other books available to him."—Daniel C. Peterson, "Mounting Evidence for the Book of Mormon," Ensign, Jan. 2000

* * *

Carrying on the legacy of the Great King Benjamin, his son Mosiah the 2nd walked in the righteous ways of his father and grandfather, and he led his people by example even tilling the land himself so that he would not be a burden to his people.

Along with his subjects, the King was also very curious about what had happened to those expeditions that had left from the city of Zarahemla to return to the land of Lehi-Nephi which was to the south of "the narrow strip of wilderness." Accordingly, he sent sixteen men led by a strong young man named Ammon the 1st who was a Mulekite, "a strong and mighty man", and a descendant of King Zarahemla. This young man also had good leadership qualities and presumably he must have had a great sense of adventure. (Mosiah 7:3)

He led his men south, wandering for forty days into the wilderness where they pitched their tents. Then he and three of his men continued on from there where they were captured, bound, and imprisoned in the land of Nephi by the guards of a Nephite King named Limhi, who happened to be traveling with his men outside the city on that particular day. Two days later, Ammon and his men were brought before King Limhi. This King Limhi identified himself as the son of King Noah and the grandson of Zeniff, the same Zeniff who had formerly led a group out of Zarahemla to re-inherit this land nearly 80 years before. Ammon then being permitted to speak explained to King Limhi that he and his men had actually been sent from Zarahemla to find out what had happened to this very same Zeniff and his people. With this news, King Limhi and his people rejoiced for they thought that Ammon and his men would deliver them from bondage, as well as the grievous taxes and the heavy rule of the Lamanites who now controlled the land of Nephi.

King Limhi then asked Ammon to bring the rest of his men into the city for food and rest. He then caused that his people should gather around to listen while Ammon "rehearsed" all that had happened in Zarahemla since his grandfather Zeniff had left the great city. After that enlightening history, King Limhi then brought before Ammon the twenty-four Gold Plates that Limhi's men had discovered in "the land of desolation" during a failed expedition to the north to find Zarahemla. They had also brought back with them the corroded swords and the brass breastplates of the long dead warriors of a mysterious ancient people, long since destroyed. (see Mosiah 8: 9-11)

In response to Limhi's beseeching of a translation for the records, Ammon then told Limhi about King Mosiah the 2nd who had a gift from God and would be able to translate the curious plates while he used the divine aide of the "interpreters." Limhi was filled with joy, as he was very desirous to know what had caused the mighty destruction of these ancient ones. (Mosiah chapters 8:12-13)

At this time, the records of King Limhi's grandfather Zeniff were also brought forth for Ammon to read. They recorded the history of Zeniff in the beginning at the time he had left Zarahemla in about 200 B.C. to the present. This all had happened about 80 years before Ammon had found these living descendants of Zeniff.

Mosiah chapter 9: through chapter 22: is the record of Zeniff and his people written in Zeniff's own words. A driven man, Zeniff had originally traveled to the land of Nephi with an army of Nephite spies to scout and assess the possibility of attacking the Lamanites. When Zeniff told his own leader that there was some good among the Lamanites and that these people should not be attacked, his unsympathetic leader commanded that Zeniff should be the one to be slain. A violent civil dispute arose in defense of Zeniff and the biggest part of the Nephite army of spies was killed in that fight. The survivors returned to Zarahemla to tell of the sorrowful, if not very stupid and very unnecessary incident. (Mosiah 9:1-2)

Zeniff was certainly not satisfied with the way things had turned out on this first expedition and he still had a desire to go back to the land southward among the Lamanites. So he gathered up another group of Nephites who also were desirous to inherit the land of their fathers and he and his followers traveled many days in the wilderness until they arrived at the borders of the land of Lehi-Nephi south of the "narrow strip of wilderness." There they camped at the same spot where the previous group from Zarahemla had been engaged in the violent and deadly dispute. A short time later, Zeniff with four of his men went on into the city where the Lamanite King ruled.

The King at first seemed very accommodating as Zeniff explained that they just wanted a little bit of the land that had belonged to their ancestors, their original inheritance where they could live in peace. Zeniff in his own words admitted that he was "overzealous" in his desire "to inherit the land of our fathers" and therefore he fell into the plot that the Lamanite King had to lull them into a false sense of security and then subject Zeniff and his people to heavy taxes and bondage. The treaty was made and Zeniff's people began to construct buildings, to repair the walls of the city of Lehi-Nephi, to till the land, raise all manner of fruit and vegetables, and "multiply and prosper in the land." (Mosiah: 9)

About twelve years later, when Zeniff's people were well established in that land, King Laman began to worry that Zeniff's people were getting too strong and that soon, he would not be able to put them in bondage and confiscate their property and riches. So he began to stir up his people against Zeniff, even raiding and slaying some of Zeniff's people in the outlaying areas. This began a war in which over three thousand Lamanites were killed and nearly three hundred of Zeniff's people. After about twenty-eight years of righteous leadership and constantly contending with the Lamanites, Zeniff growing old and tired turned the Kingdom over to his son, Noah.

Noah, as a scriptural understatement says, "did not walk in the ways of his father." As the new King of the Nephites in that land, Noah broke all the commandments, and caused his people to wallow in sin and commit whoredoms and all manner of abominations, and he taxed them heavily so he could support his many wives and concubines. His people following the example of their leader, drank much wine, began to worship idols, and delighted in the shedding of blood. The Nephite Kingdom in the original land of Nephi was in a sad state of affairs and seemed to closely resemble a Nephite version of Sodom and Gomorrah.

"And it came to pass," among the very few righteous Nephites that were left in the community, a prophet named Abinadi stepped forward. He told the people in no uncertain words that unless they repented and soon, that they would be delivered into the hands of their enemies and brought into bondage from which no one but the Lord could deliver them. The people were incensed by the prophet Abinadi's words and wanted to slay him.

King Noah was also much disturbed by Abinadi's words, and he commanded that Abinadi be captured and brought before him. Strangely enough, Abinadi managed to evade his pursuers for two years. They finally found him, bound him, and took him before King Noah and then they tattled, saying that Abinadi had said that the King's life wasn't worth "a garment in a furnace of fire" because of his great iniquities. King Noah was more than a little perturbed and had Abinadi thrown in prison. He then commanded that his council of priest aid him in deciding how to punish the prophet Abinadi. The council requested that the accused be brought before them for questioning so that they might convict him with his own words. This didn't go quite as well as they had planned, as Abinadi fended off their trick questions with skill, wisdom, and truth, and probably more than a little help from the Lord. He also reminded them of their great heritage and their glaring failure to teach righteousness to the people.

King Noah exclaimed to his priest "He is mad" therefore take him away and slay him. As the priest tried to lay their hands upon him, Abinadi shouted "Touch me not, for God shall smite you if you lay your hands upon me, for I have not delivered the message which the Lord sent me to deliver . . ." They did not dare touch him! He then continued his message and reviewed the Ten Commandments with them, quoting much from Isaiah, and again reminded them of their failures to teach righteousness.

King Noah immediately demanded that the priest take him and put him to death. The prophet Abinadi's words had fallen upon deaf ears and many hardened hearts, except for one lone priest who just happened to be a direct descendent of Nephi the 1st. His name was Alma, a priest of Noah, true, but now with a mighty change wrought upon his heart and soul.

(Mosiah 17:2) (Mosiah 11,12,13)

The words of Abinadi had touched Alma the 1st like none before and he knew in his heart that Abinadi was a true prophet of the Lord. He therefore pleaded for Abinadi's life before King Noah. This only enraged the King and he sent his servants to slay Alma. Consequently, Alma had to flee for his own life. When he finally found a good and safe hiding place, he remembered, pondered, and wrote down the prophetic words of Abinadi, which had changed his life forever.

Meanwhile, the wicked King Noah decided to throw Abinadi in prison for three days before he pronounced his final sentence. The King almost changed his mind when Abinadi convincingly declared to him that the judgments of God would surely be upon his head, but the wicked priest swayed King Noah's decision in the other direction, all to the doomed prophet's misfortune. The prophet Abinadi was then burned to death, even as he prophesied that the wicked among them would suffer the same punishment, culminating in a cruel and most painful death, a death by fire.

*   *   *

CHAPTER SEVEN

* * *

ALL ROADS LEAD TO ZARAHEMLA

Alma the 1st, a former priest of King Noah, but now having repented and dedicating himself to serve God, fled before the servants of the wicked King Noah in the land of Nephi. He thus escaped, and having repented of his sins was now teaching his humble followers all the words of the prophet Abinadi as they hid in secret places while trying to avoid the King's men. Several hundred believers followed him into the wilderness to a place called Mormon. At a spot, which was nearby the thickets and trees where they hid in the daytime, was "a fountain of pure water" which they called "The waters of Mormon." Alma, "having the authority of Almighty God" did baptize himself and his first convert, Helam, as they buried themselves in the water together. He then proceeded to baptize the next convert but without immersing himself, and continued going down into the water until he had baptized two hundred and two souls in all. (Mosiah 18:14-16) Being that he now had authority from God, he also ordained priests to teach them, one priest for every fifty souls, and he did therefore organize "The Church of Christ."

When the King became aware of the suspicious movement among the people, he deployed spies who then reported that Alma and his followers were now hiding at the Waters of Mormon. The

King's army was soon sent to find them, because the paranoid King Noah was sure that they were stirring up rebellion against him, and thus he ordered their execution. Fortunately, Alma and his followers were tipped off and so they did gather up their families and belongings and fled deep into the wilderness being led by their spiritual leader Alma, and the good graces of the Lord. There were about four hundred and fifty of them. (Mosiah 18:32-34)

Meanwhile, there were other dissenters among King Noah's people. One of them was adamant in his opposition towards the King, and he was a strong man in body and spirit. This man called Gideon was a righteous man and was well aware of the predominant cause of the wickedness among his people and therefore was determined to execute the despicable King Noah. He confronted the King with sword in hand and in an attitude that was determined to put an end to the king's wicked ways, but his plans were unexpectedly disrupted at the disarming sighting of Lamanite soldiers within the borders of the land.

Saved by the bell from Gideon's wrath, the frightened King Noah ordered his people to flee, but the Lamanite soldiers soon caught up with them and began to slay them without mercy. King Noah then commanded that all of his men should flee for their lives and at least try to save themselves, even as they left behind their defenseless wives and children. In a panic, some of the men, however reluctant they may have felt, abandoned their families and did flee with King Noah and his wicked priests, while some of them stayed with their wives and children to face the Lamanite warriors. The ones, who stayed, were glad they did because the Lamanites took compassion upon them due to the pleading of their fair Nephite daughters.

The Lamanites let most of the Nephites return to their homes for a tribute of one half of all their property and gold. Even though they were still subject to the overall rule of their conquers, the Nephites were now under the immediate leadership of their own nominal King Limhi. Even though he was the son of the nefarious King Noah, he was basically a just and good ruler, and he did not walk in the questionable ways of his father.

Meanwhile, the Nephite patriot, Gideon, sent men into the wilderness to find King Noah and his wicked priests. Instead they found the sorrowful and repentant men who had fled with the King at the expense of their own families. These men then reported how King Noah had commanded them to not return to their families even after they had sorrowfully repented of their regrettable deed. They were so angry with King Noah that they took him and burned him to death, fulfilling Abinadi's prophecy.

The surviving wicked priests then fled further into the wilderness to save their own miserable lives, while the repentant Nephite men returned home to find their wives and children alive and well. In spite of the fact that the Lamanites leveled a 50% tax upon them, and kept a 24-hour guard surrounding the Nephites, never the less, under the leadership of their own Nephite King Limhi, the Nephite people lived a reasonably good life and a life of peace for the next two years.

The wicked priests of King Noah, not daring to go home, wandered in the wilderness. During their wandering, they happened upon twenty and four of the daughters of the Lamanites who were singing and dancing in the wilderness, which we can probably assume was more forest like rather than what we normally picture as a dry barren desert like wilderness. Since the wicked priests didn't dare return to their own families, they decided to kidnap the Lamanite daughters and make these young women their new wives.

When the Lamanites discovered their daughters were missing, they just presumed it was the people of Limhi who had taken them. So they attacked Limhi's people, in spite of the oath that they had made to let them live in peace. During the fierce battle, the wounded Lamanite King was captured and taken before King Limhi, who of course, knew nothing about the girls being carried away. Then Gideon, Limhi's wise captain, stepped forth and reminded King Limhi of the wicked priests still in the forest somewhere who had never returned. Might they be the culprits? It all made sense, and the King of the Lamanites was appeased, persuaded his people to not attack again, and they returned to their own lands in peace. (Mosiah 20)

Meanwhile King Limhi and his people kept watch for the wicked priests who had caused so much trouble. When Ammon the 1st and his men of the expedition from Zarahemla wandered into the land of Nephi, Limhi's men thought they might be part of the wicked priests of Noah, and so bound them and took them before King Limhi to answer for their crimes.

King Limhi listened to their explanation, and then being a just and good man, despite his wicked father's legacy, was soon converted by Ammon and so he gave Ammon access to all their records including the twenty-four gold plates as previously noted. King Limhi's people were also very receptive to Ammon's missionary efforts and did covet to obey the Lord's commandments and they all were desirous to be baptized. Neither Ammon nor any of his men had the authority to baptize, so it was decided that somehow, someway, the people had to escape from the bondage of the Lamanites.

Limhi's wise Captain Gideon then stepped forth with a plan. They would pay tribute to the Lamanite guards at the back of the city with plenty of wine, which the Lamanite guards would drink freely without to much persuasion. When the guards were good and drunk, then all of the people with all of their animals, and all of their goods, would pass through the back pass and escape into the wilderness. King Limhi and Ammon supported Gideon's idea fully and the plan was carried out without a hitch.

Now safely and quietly freed from the Lamanites, Ammon the 1st and his men led Limhi's people many days through the wilderness until they finally arrived in Zarahemla. King Mosiah the 2nd received them and their records with great joy, as they became his newest subjects in the land of Zarahemla. (Mosiah 22:)

So then what happened to Alma the 1st and his followers? Well, after they ran from King Noah's army, they fled into the wilderness for eight days, still to the south of the narrow strip of wilderness. There they made a new home, built buildings, tilled the ground, and became very industrious. They called their new home, the land of Helam and built a great city there, which was also called Helam, and they did prosper greatly in the new land.

Unfortunately, the Lamanite army who had unsuccessfully tried to catch up with and recapture King Limhi and his escaping people were still wandering around in the wilderness. By happenstance, they stumbled upon the wicked priests of King Noah and the kidnapped Lamanite daughters, which they had forced to be their wives. The Lamanite daughters pleaded with the Lamanites warriors to not kill these wicked priests who were now their husbands and the fathers of their babies and young children. Obviously some time had passed since the wicked priests had first kidnapped the girls, made them to be their wives, and had children with them. The sacred record keepers often recorded events without specific time references or without specifying the amount of time that had passed from one event to the next.

The Lamanites soldiers had compassion upon the Lamanite daughters and so let them and the wicked priests along with their wicked leader, a man called Amulon, join up with the Lamanite army. United into one group, they all proceeded to travel through the wilderness seeking the land of Nephi, but instead stumbled into the land of Helam where Alma the 1st and his followers were now living. It was a tense situation, but the Lamanites were in an awkward position too, and so promised they would give Alma and his people their liberty if he would but show them the way back to the land of Nephi. Alma did so, but the Lamanites not only lied about giving them their liberty, but also to make matters even worse, made the wicked priest Amulon the new King and ruler over the land of Helam and Alma's people. (Mosiah 23)

Amulon, having once been a dedicated leader among King Noah's wicked priests, considered Alma to be a very much-despised traitor to him and the other priests. With his newfound power over Alma and his people, he delighted in making their lives miserable, even commanding that they be put to death if they were caught praying. Never the less, they continued to pray in their hearts with great faith, and their burdens were lightened. So great was their faith that "the voice of the Lord came unto them", saying that they would be delivered from their awful bondage. (Mosiah 24:16)

Soon after this, Alma and his people gathered their flocks, their grains, and all their goods together, and then early the next morning while the Lamanite guards and all the taskmasters were in a deep sleep caused by the Lord, the people of Alma escaped and departed into the wilderness led by Alma under the guidance of the Lord. Traveling for twelve days, they finally arrived in the great city of Zarahemla.

Just as he had received Limhi's people, King Mosiah the 2nd did receive Alma's people also with great joy. Mosiah then asked that an account of Alma's people and their afflictions should be read in a public gathering as well as the records of the people of Zeniff. King Mosiah the 2nd's own people were filled with joy at the Lords deliverance of their brethren and gave thanks to God for the blessing.

Then Mosiah prevailed upon Alma to speak to the people. Alma proceeded and reminded those who had been delivered from bondage how the Lord had helped them escape, and delivered them, and then he proceeded to teach them many righteous things. When Alma was through with his many words of inspiration, Limhi and his people desired to be baptized and so Alma went forth into the water and baptized them into the church of God.

At this time, King Mosiah the 2nd granted permission to Alma the 1st to establish churches throughout the land of Zarahemla, with each church having its own priests and teachers because of the great numbers of people in the land. But each church only taught what Alma taught them, "And thus notwithstanding there be many churches they were all one church . . ."

(Mosiah 25:22, chaps. 24 & 25)

Now it came to pass that in the great city of Zarahemla, that King Mosiah the 2nd was now the ruler over four different righteous communities of people. First there were the people of Mulek who were the original founders of Zarahemla. They had escaped from Jerusalem with Prince Mulek at the time of the Babylonian conquest. This Prince Mulek was the ancestor of King Zarahemla and the only surviving son of Zedekiah, the last Jewish King in Jerusalem. (Mosiah 25:2)

Then a second large group composed of exiled righteous Nephites came wandering into Zarahemla led by Mosiah the 1st; he having been directed to leave the land of Nephi by the Lord about 400 years after Nephi the 1st had passed away. The Lord had guided them to Zarahemla, and Mosiah the 1st became their King by popular demand, thus becoming King over the exiled Nephites and the Mulekites or the people of Zarahemla, as the Book of Mormon calls them.

In the third group came the people of King Limhi. They were descendants of the people of Zeniff, who were originally part of the Mosiah the 1st's exiled Nephites but had left Zarahemla in 200 B.C. with their leader Zeniff to re-inherit the land of Lehi-Nephi south of the narrow strip of wilderness. Over time, even though they were originally the righteous people of Zeniff, they had gradually become very wicked under King Noah's rule. Yet they were now repentant, converted, and baptized, and had finally returned to the home of their grandfathers, in the great city of Zarahemla.

And lastly, there were the people of Alma the 1st, who had been some of the very few righteous Nephites living under the rule of King Noah. They had followed Alma into wilderness after the death of the prophet Abinadi where they were baptized by Alma into the Church of Christ. They had built a whole new community in the land of Helam. Subsequently they were discovered by the Lamanite army who put them under the heavy-handed rule of Amulon, the wicked and cruel exiled priest of Noah. There they remained in bondage at Helam, right up until their miraculous escape.

Chapter 25 of Mosiah mentions an additional smaller group of people in verse 12. They were the children of the evil priest Amulon and the other wicked priest of Noah. They had become so ashamed of the conduct of their fathers that they not only rejected their fathers' ways but even their names. So now they took upon themselves the name of Nephi, as they desired to become a righteous people and be numbered among the Nephites in Zarahemla.

So it came to pass that all five of these groups were united and living together in peace, under the auspices of the last King of the Nephites. He proclaimed that there "should be no persecutions among them" but equality among all men. "That they should let no pride nor haughtiness disturb their peace; that every man should esteem his neighbor as himself, laboring with their own hands for their support." (Mosiah 27:4)

This last Nephite King, now ruling over the great communities in Zarahemla, was the son of King Benjamin, the grandson of King Mosiah the 1st, and the third King in the line of the Mosiah Dynasty. This King Mosiah the 2nd was a man of fine heritage, great integrity, much wisdom, and truly a righteous servant of the Lord, who ruled justly. Thus by 120 B.C., or 480 years after Lehi left Jerusalem, the great city of Zarahemla had become the new center of Zion and was now to be the new Nephite homeland.

*   *   *

CHAPTER EIGHT

*   *   *

THE GREAT CONVERSION AND
A NEW ERA

"And now there were seven churches in the land of Zarahemla. And it came to pass that whosoever were desirous to take upon them the name of Christ, or of God, they did join the churches of God; . . . and they were blessed and prospered in the land." (Mosiah 25: 23-24)

Nevertheless there were nonbelievers and dissenters among the righteous; even King Mosiah the 2nd's own sons, Ammon, Aaron, Omner and Himni, as well as their good friend, Alma the 2nd, who was the prophet Alma's son. He was also known as Alma the younger. These five dissidents, Alma the younger and the four sons of Mosiah rebelled against their parent's wishes and against the accepted moral and ethical behavior of their community. Perhaps being like many young people of today, they had to prove that they had a right to think differently from their parents and the right to choose wrong if they so desired, and the right to be rebellious despite the consequences, even if it meant going against their parent's teachings.

Alma the younger is described as being "a very wicked and an idolatrous man" who spoke much flattery to the people and led them away causing much dissension among them, even hindering the prosperity of the church. He and the sons of Mosiah went about secretly attempting to lead people astray and were actually trying to destroy the church. Needless to say, this was not pleasing to their fathers or to their God.

On one particular and fateful occasion, as they were going about their rebellious ways, an angel of the Lord appeared to them, speaking to them, astonishing them, causing them to actually fall upon the ground, then saying to Alma in a voice like unto thunder, the words which were somewhat like that said to the Apostle Paul; "Why persecutest thou the church of God?" The angel proceeded then to tell Alma the younger that because of the faith and prayers of his own father, the prophet Alma, that he the angel had now been sent to convince the younger Alma of the power and the authority of God so that the prayers of his father and the people could be answered.

Needless to say, the angel made an impression upon them and thus had their full attention at this point, and Alma was so struck that he could not speak or move. Momentarily recovering from their great astonishment, the sons of Mosiah carried the nearly comatose and helpless Alma to his father. Not having the normal expected very concerned reaction, Alma's father was overjoyed, knowing that it was the hand of the Lord that had done this, and he assembled the people and the priests to pray for his son. After two days of fasting and praying by the priests, having been requested to do so by Alma's father, Alma began to receive strength to his arms and legs and he then spoke. He then said how he had repented of his sins, been redeemed of the Lord, and had been born of the spirit; "My soul was racked with eternal torment; but I am snatched and my soul is pained no more." (Mosiah 27:29)

From that day on, Alma the 2nd having fully repented of his old and misguided ways tried to undo the bad that he had done, and he went about doing good and teaching the people in the ways of righteousness. Unbeknownst to him in his current state of reform, he would eventually become one of the greatest missionaries of the entire Book of Mormon.

The sons of Mosiah, having also truly repented, also went about trying to undo the damage that they had done, explaining to their listeners about the prophecies and scriptures, and preaching "knowledge of their Redeemer" among the people. They even drafted some of the people as missionaries, and then returned to their father with a request that was not well received by their father. They told him that they wished to go into the land of Nephi and preach to the people there. This particular land where they wished to do missionary work was to the south of the "narrow strip of wilderness" and was the former Nephite "land of inheritance" originally settled by their ancestors, the original land of Father Lehi and his family. It was now totally overrun and controlled by the violent, wicked, and unbelieving Lamanites. This state of affairs in the "land of inheritance" was the very situation that Jacob, the brother of Nephi, had prophesied and warned his people about, as he told them what would happen if the Nephite people were not obedient and repentant. Thus this warning had become a reality, and had become an unfortunate and inevitable consequence of their sins. Nevertheless, this was the very place that the sons of King Mosiah the 2nd desired that they should go, so that they might bring the word of God to the wild and spiritually lost Lamanites; and yes, to save their very souls.

King Mosiah, being a loving and concerned father, was not especially happy with their request, but did not want to stifle their good intentions, so he inquired of the Lord as what to do. The Lord told Mosiah the 2nd that many Lamanites would believe on his sons' words, and that his sons would be protected from harm while they delivered the word of the Lord in the Land of Nephi. So King Mosiah gave into their righteous desires and granted permission for his beloved sons to leave on their dangerous and most challenging missions. (Mosiah 28)

Meanwhile, being that there were none of his sons who wanted to take over for their father as the new King, King Mosiah the 2nd gathered the plates of brass, the plates of Nephi, the Jaredite plates of gold which he had translated for his people, and the other sacred objects, including the interpreters, and he conferred them upon Alma the younger and commanded him that he should keep and preserve these things.

Although the people had expressed their desire to King Mosiah that his son Aaron should be their new King, King Mosiah convinced them that with the situation being that none of his sons wanted to be king, they should not have any king rule over them. He then reminded them that kings could not always be trusted to do good for their people, as he cited the infamous case of the wicked King Noah. He therefore suggested that they should consider a system of judges. The people were delighted with this suggestion and the liberty that it gave them, and so they did choose a system of judges to rule over them according to the laws of the land. One of the judges that they chose to rule and judge them, just happened to be the now repentant Alma the 2nd, previously known as Alma the younger, and yes, the previously "Holy Terror" of Zarahemla. Although Alma the younger had already had the burden of being chief high priest of the church conferred upon him by his father, the people of Zarahemla now chose Alma the younger to be their first chief judge, the historic first chief judge of all the Nephite people.

The time period was now five hundred and nine years since Lehi left Jerusalem. Alma the elder, "having gone the way of all the earth" and having fulfilled the commandments of God, was gone at age 82. King Mosiah the 2nd then passed away at 63 in the 33rd year of his righteous and just reign, and thus the great reign of kings had come to an end among the Nephite people in about 91 years before the birth of Christ.

Alma the younger, as the first chief judge did walk in the ways of his father and he did keep the commandments of the Lord and he made righteous judgments for the people. He upheld the laws established by King Mosiah the 2nd, and promoted peace throughout the lands of the Nephites. (Mosiah 29)

However, in his very first year as chief judge, Alma soon found out that even when most of the people are righteous and active in the church, there will always arise a few obstinate individuals who are in opposition to almost every thing that good people try to do, and of course, they will inevitably present more trials for the faithful.

A large and strong man named Nehor, dressed in costly apparel, began to preach false doctrine among the people, teaching them that they would all be redeemed and saved no matter how they conducted their lives, regardless of their many sins. He told them it was of no consequence whether they were righteous or not; it did not matter, because they were going to go to heaven no matter how they lived their lives. In reality, he was telling them a partial truth that all men would be saved from death by the atonement of Christ. He wasn't telling them that they would still have to be judged and receive an appropriate reward according to how they lived on earth. He went on to say that all priests, such as himself, should be completely supported by donations from the people. There were many who found his philosophy very appealing and believed in his words, and so they did give him money.

When Limhi's former captain Gideon confronted Nehor about his false teachings, the wicked Nehor struck him down and killed him with his sword and showed the aging Gideon no mercy what so ever. Nehor was immediately taken before Alma the 2nd to be judged. Alma pointed out Nehor's grievous crimes, namely murder and priest craft, and sentenced him to death according to the laws of the land. He was then taken to the hill Manti and promptly and justifiably executed.

Unfortunately, this did not put an end to what Nehor had been teaching, and soon there were many preaching similar false doctrines for the sake of riches, honor, and personal gain. These same individuals began to persecute members of the church; arguing and contending "even unto blows." Consequently, their names were blotted out from the church, as they committed thievery, whoredoms, sorcery, and even murder, and they would establish what would eventually become the infamous, the destructive, and the evil "order of Nehors."

Nevertheless, the majority of the people were trying to live the commandments, as they gave to the poor, took care of the needy and the afflicted, and prospered in general peace until the fifth year of the reign of the judges. (Alma chap. 1)

At that time, a cunning man called Amlici (am li si), who followed the same beliefs as the order of Nehor, began to flatter and persuade many people that it was a good idea to do away with the system of judges and establish him as their wise and powerful king. He beguiled so many that a public vote was forced upon the people to put an end to the chaotic political unrest, but quite unexpectedly to him "The voice of the people came against Amlici."

However, this did not dissuade Amlici or his supporters. He had so many followers that they consecrated him as their king and took upon themselves the name of "Amlicites." Amlici then commanded them to arm themselves and attack the people of God, to force them to be his subjects. But the righteous Nephites were able to organize well under the leadership of Alma, and not only defended themselves, but "they slew the Amlicites with great slaughter." After losing 12,532 men, the Amlicites fled in fear, but not for long. Nephite scouts soon discovered the Amlicites had joined up with Lamanite invaders and were preparing to come against the Nephite people, once again. (Alma 2:16-18)

While the Nephite army was crossing the river Sidon, heading back to Zarahemla, the combined Amlicite and Lamanite armies ambushed them with great numbers ". . . as the sands of the sea." Despite the odds, the Nephites were "strengthened by the hand of the Lord" and the enemy did fall before them. During the battle, Alma the 2nd met the devious Amlici face-to-face and with faith and prayer and sword in hand, he was able to slay Amlici. He also contended with the fleeing Lamanite King, who fled and escaped, but in the end the Amlicite and Lamanite armies were soundly defeated. The dead at the river Sidon were washed out to sea to have their bones buried in the water's cold depths. The wounded surviving Lamanites scattered and fled to the wilderness of Hermounts north and west of the river Sidon. In a very grizzly ending, this is the place where "wild and ravenous beast" and "the vultures of the air" devoured so many of the Lamanites. (Alma 2:)

The surviving Amlicites marked their foreheads with red to distinguish themselves from the hated Nephites, not realizing they were fulfilling the word of God, as He had told Nephi that those who mingled with the Lamanites would have a mark set upon them and be cursed also. These fallen apostate Nephites had "come out in open rebellion against God" and they brought upon themselves the consequences, condemnation, and the inevitable justice that was entailed in the "curse" of the Lamanites.

Some time later, a second Lamanite army tried to come against the Nephites in the fifth year of the reign of judges. Alma who did not participate directly in the battle because of his still healing wounds, sent out a large army that was able to easily defeat the Lamanites a second time, and the Nephites enjoyed relative peace once again, for awhile. (Alma 3:)

*   *   *

CHAPTER NINE

* * *

THEN THE MISSIONARY YEARS

After the Lamanites and their Amlicite cohorts were defeated, there was peace in the land for the time being. However, the people did lament for some time over the loss of so many lives and all the property losses due to the war. This humbled them and they sought refuge in the Lord. Consequently, thousands were baptized into the church by Alma the 2nd. The newly converted members began to prosper and they did continue faithfully in the church for a while. Yet, as little as one year later, in the eighth year of the reign of the judges, the populous began to be caught up in the pursuit of riches and costly apparel, and in the pride of their fine herds of livestock. Soon there was much self-pride prevalent among the people. In their arrogance, they began to discriminate against the less fortunate, even to the point that they persecuted the poor and turned their backs on the needy who they had judged to be not acceptable nor wanted in the general community. All of this brought much contention and unrest into the church and set a very bad example for the non-members among them.

Alma became disheartened and somewhat discouraged by this sad state of his people. The wearing of two hats and his many responsibilities became nearly overwhelming to him and he was nearly exhausted from the burden. So he resigned from the judgment seat and then proceeded to select a good and wise man to be the new chief judge of the Nephites. He was one of the elders of the church, and his name was Nephihah. (Alma 4:)

Alma, then no longer being encumbered by the chief judge position, but still having retained the office of chief high priest, went among the people "that he might preach the word of God unto them" and he reminded them of their duties as he sought to deliver them from their own pride and iniquity. As he started to see positive results being made from his well-directed efforts, he turned over the church in Zarahemla to the priests and elders that he had ordained and given authority to, and then he left for a new and more challenging field of harvest.

He headed east to the city of Gideon on the other side of the river Sidon. Speaking to them with the spirit of prophecy, which was in him, he told them of the Christ child which would be born to Mary, a glorious Savior for all of mankind. He spoke of humility, faith, hope, and charity. He warned them of walking in crooked paths, and urged them to be "temperate in all things." When he felt that the church in Gideon was well on a path to righteousness, he left it in the hands of the proper order of the priesthood of the church, and then returned to the great city of Zarahemla to take a break from his missionary efforts.

The next year, after a good rest, he headed west to the other side of the river Sidon to the land of Melek on the edge of the wilderness. There he preached, converted, and baptized. Having good success in Melek, he then headed north, traveling for three days, to a city called Ammonihah. Unfortunately, Satan had already beaten him there. The people were hard hearted and they told Alma in no uncertain terms that they didn't believe in the foolishness that he was preaching, and that since he was no longer chief judge of the land, he had no business even bothering them with his high minded preaching. They reviled him, spit upon him and threw him out of the city.

Needless to say, being dejected, rejected, and ejected, he felt sorrowful and certainly disillusioned. Therefore, feeling somewhat down and discouraged, he decided to try another city called Aaron. On the way there, he was approached by an angel of the Lord, which more or less "gave him a pat on the back" for his faithfulness, but then pointedly commanded him to return to the city of Ammonihah to warn its people to repent or be destroyed. Obediently and with haste, Alma returned to Ammonihah, only this time by another route coming in from the south end of the city.

He met a stranger who he implored saying; "Will ye give to an humble servant of God something to eat?" The stranger who's name was Amulek, had already seen Alma in a vision, and had been told by an angel that Alma was a holy prophet, and thus he was commanded to take care of him. So Amulek took Alma to his own home and fed him bread and meat. Alma ate, thanked his God, blessed Amulek and his family, blessed their home, and explained his purpose and mission in Ammonihah. (Alma 8:)

After a good rest and having tarried with Amulek several days, Alma the 2nd, having been commanded by God, took Amulek as his missionary companion, and went among the wicked people of Ammonihah and began to preach repentance unto them again. They didn't receive the good word and warning any better this time than the last time, and again contended with him with great rudeness. He warned them that because of their heritage, and their teachings, and their many opportunities to repent, it would be more tolerable for the Lamanites than them, and that unless they repented, they would be absolutely and completely destroyed by the Lamanites. The people, thus angry and greatly annoyed by this damning revelation, tried to throw Alma in prison, but "the Lord did not suffer them" that they should.

Alma's missionary companion, Amulek, being inspired, then took his turn at preaching the good message and he spoke many words to the people. He recounted his own heritage back through Nephi even to Joseph who was sold into Egypt. He admitted that he had had a hardened heart and a lack of belief in the Lord at one time in his life, but then that had all changed. He recounted the story of his encounter with an angel of the Lord, and how it had changed his whole attitude and spirit. He enthusiastically emphasized his own strong testimony and he fervently declared that Alma was and is truly a holy man of God and that the things that he spoke are the words of truth.

The people were angry with him and reviled him, but he countered boldly and accused them of being a "perverse generation" whose foundation of destruction would be laid down by their unrighteous lawyers and judges.

Wicked lawyers among the people tried to "cross his words" that they might condemn him according to their own laws. They were led by an expert lawyer who had a greedy evil spirit and a deceiving tongue. This lawyer went by the name of Zeezrom. The design of Zeezrom and his fellow lawyers was to deliberately stir up contention among the people so that they could practice their craft and receive their wages according to the law, even if it was only a temporary settlement of disputes. Of course, all this was for a nice healthy fee. Zeezrom was an expert at his craft. He started in on Amulek, even offering him a substantial amount of silver if Amulek would but deny the existence of God.

To say that Amulek chastised the cunning Zeezrom is an understatement. Amulek called him a "child of hell" and accused him of loving money more than God. Seemingly undaunted, Zeezrom continued with his trick questions, but Amulek, unwavering in his faith and spirit, deftly fended off Zeezrom's trick questions with profound statements of religious truth concerning the nature of God, the eternal plan, and men's death and immortality.

Then taking over for Amulek, Alma proceeded with inspired statements of truth concerning the mysteries of God and the plan of redemption, which started to have an unexpected effect on Zeezrom, even to the point that he began to think Alma and Amulek could see into his heart and mind. Then in an amazing turn of events, almost miraculously, Zeezrom began to have a true change of heart and mind. He shockingly began to ask sincere questions so that he might know more about the kingdom of God. Alma eloquently expounded upon the subject. Alma spoke of Abraham, Melchizedek, and the holy priesthood, and finally concluded with admonishments of repentance. Zeezrom along with some of the other people who heard the words of Alma and Amulek were actually converted to the truth of the Gospel. However, there were a great many more who were incensed by their own heart pricking guilt and they did reject the two missionaries.

When Zeezrom tried to reason with the guilty ones and defend the two prophets, the unrepentant people did cast out from among them Zeezrom and the other believers. They also took and bound Alma and Amulek and forced them to watch, as the wicked people and their lawyers burned to death many of the innocent believers along with their records and scriptures. Amulek watching in horror asked Alma, "How can we witness this awful scene?" And not "exercise the power of God which is in us and save them from the flames." (Alma 14:10) Alma being constrained by the spirit said that this painful scene must be allowed to happen without interference in order that "the blood of the innocent shall stand as a witness" against the wicked.

Shortly thereafter, the judges and lawyers after the order of Nehor proceeded to abuse Alma and Amulek in prison for many days, taunting them, spitting on them and smiting them. The chief judge rudely challenged the missionaries proclaiming that they did not have the power to save the innocent. He proclaimed that even their own God didn't have the power to save the ones that were cast into the fire, so just how was Amulek and Alma going to save themselves, let alone save any one else.

In desperation, Alma cried unto the Lord for deliverance. As the cords with which they were bound broke, the earth shook and the walls of the prison trembled, twisted, and fell into a pile of rubble crushing all the arrogant wicked tormentors within the walls and they were killed and buried in the rubble. Alma and Amulek then walked forth from the prison without a scratch, while the witnesses fled in great fear, "as a goat fleeth with her young from two lions." (Alma 14:)

After this traumatic but miraculous experience, Alma and Amulek were commanded by God to leave Ammonihah and go to the land of Sidom. There they would find the few righteous people of Ammonihah who had been cast out from their homes who were now hiding in refuge.

The newly repentant Zeezrom was residing with these refugees. He was sick with a fever, which was caused by a great and overwhelming guilt as he supposed that Alma and Amulek had already been slain and he had been the cause. When he heard that they were alive and well, and now in Sidom, he rejoiced and sent for them as he himself was unable to get out of bed. On their arrival, he stretched out his hand pleading that the two missionaries would please heal him.

After questioning him and determining his faith in the redemption of Christ, Alma was satisfied with his true repentance and therefore had compassion upon him crying unto the Lord; "O Lord our God, have mercy on this man, and heal him according to his faith which is in Christ." (Alma 15:10) Through the power of Alma's priesthood, Zeezrom "leaped upon his feet and began to walk." He astonished the witnesses who then spread the word of the miracle throughout the land. The time was now right and Alma baptized Zeezrom who became a righteous preacher unto the people. Meanwhile Alma established a church, consecrated priest and teachers, and baptized "flocks" of new converts. Alma the 2nd was very pleased and satisfied with the way the Lord's work was progressing.

Amulek, Alma's faithful missionary companion, having been rejected by his kindred in Ammonihah, gave up his gold and silver and the other precious things of his former life, and returned with Alma to the great city of Zarahemla, thus ending the tenth year of the reign of judges over the people of Nephi.

Looking at the other side of the coin during these events, the truly wicked people in Ammonihah did not repent. They even attributed the miracles of Alma and Amulek to the devil, and they remained hardhearted and faithful to the profession of Nehor, which eventually brought about their own demise and complete destruction.

In the eleventh year of the reign of judges, Alma's warning became a reality and the cry of war came upon the land and the Lamanites attacked the Nephite city of Ammonihah. They slew these wicked unrepentant Nephites as Alma had prophesied, and destroyed the city, and took many captives, just as Alma and Amulek had warned these stubborn people.

The faithful Nephite Chief Captain Zoram the 2nd, knowing that Alma had the spirit of prophecy, inquired of the High Priest as to what the Lord would have the Nephite armies do. After praying, Alma received specific instructions from the Lord as to how Zoram and his men should meet the Lamanite warriors at a certain crossing on the river Sidon, and there the Lord would deliver the captive Nephites into their hands. Captain Zoram and his two sons, along with the Nephite army did meet the Lamanites there, scattered them and drove them into the wilderness. The Nephite captives were recovered and delivered to their own lands and homes.

Even though things had gone well for Chief Captain Zoram, and he certainly had been victorious at the river Sidon, meanwhile, there were surviving Lamanites warriors who had their own plans and a vengeful desire to attack and murder all the Nephite people that were left in the wicked city of Ammonihah and so they did. "In one day it was left desolate; and the carcasses were mangled by dogs and wild beast of the wilderness."

Ironically, the wicked Nephite people of Ammoniha had boasted that even God could not destroy their city, because of its greatness. Their empty boast ended in the total annihilation of the city of Ammonihah by the Lamanite armies, thus fulfilling Alma's prophecy that their Lamanite enemies would bring about the "utter destruction" of the unrepentant people of Ammonihah. The extermination was so complete that the stench of the heaped up bodies upon the land remained for years, and the rest of the people throughout the area avoided the land of Ammonihah, as no one wanted to possess its filth and stench. Because the wicked people of Ammonihah had stubbornly insisted on following the profession of the evil Nehor, their city was completely destroyed and their homeland became known as the "Desolation of Nehors." (Alma 16:11)

*   *   *

So many great cities in the history of the world, such as Rome, Athens, Alexandria, Babylon, Jericho, Jerusalem, Sodom and Gomorrah, Zarahemla, and even the great Aztec city of Tenochtitlan, have all thought that their cities were so great that they were invincible and could not be destroyed. All were wrong. No people, however great they think they may be, can ignore God's commandments and continue to wallow in their own wickedness without there eventually being a heavy price to be paid.

Is there some kind of a profound warning in all these very convincing and undeniable consequences throughout history, incontestable evidence of the eventual justice for the wicked that ignore God's commandments? Does history really repeat itself over and over? In our modern day society, can we believe that we can continue in the degradation of our morals and our integrity without there eventually being consequences?

It only takes a brief amount of observation to see that our news media, television, popular music, and movie entertainment, all illustrate that our overall morals as a society are in fast decline. How often do we look around, and see the pervasive drug and alcohol abuse every where we look, blatant immoral activities, riotous weekend partying, rampant crime and uncontrolled gang activity in our big cities, astonishing sums of money lost to white collar fraud, embezzlement, and those insidious "ponzie" schemes. Vast political corruption and government fraud seems to be ignored by the law, while the ubiquitous con artist is trying every conceivable way to take money from the innocent, the elderly, and the naïve. All this is frightening evidence that sadly reveals that we as a nation are walking much too close to the edge.

*   *   *

Encyclopedia of Mormonism, Vol.4, WRATH OF GOD

"God's wrath may come upon individuals or nations or civilizations when they have 'ripened in iniquity.' His wrath manifests itself most completely when a majority of the people desire that which is contrary to the laws of God and have already chosen iniquity for themselves. The people of Noah's day, the people of Ammonihah, the Jaredites, the Nephites, and to a small degree, the Latter-day Saints in Missouri all experienced God's wrath in their time."

*   *   *

Is there anything we can we do as individuals? We certainly can't change the trend of the world, but we can make a difference among our families and friends and neighbors. That small minority of the faithful in the wicked city of Ammonihah was saved from the wrath of God due to their righteousness and they were delivered to a place of refuge and hope. Our own communities can be places of refuge and hope, if we work at it, and stand strong as a unified force supporting each other against the great many wrongs of the world around us. We must not give up in the face of what seems like a world gone mad. We can make a difference in our own communities, setting examples, being active voters, and active volunteers in supporting the good things in our part of the community.

We must lovingly teach and be an example of spiritual strength to our families and "Train up a child in the way he should go: and when he is old, he will not depart from it." (Prov. 22: 6) A great many faithful parents have discovered that even if their children do stray for a while, even completely rejecting their parents and their religion, many will eventually make a complete turn around. With the example of righteous teachings set deep in the back of their young minds, combined with the daily prayers of their parents, most of these wayward children will some day see the futility of living an immoral unprincipled life without direction and come wandering back to the safety of the fold and their teachings. They eventually will discover that a true feeling of security can only come in this life by living in the way that we know that our Heavenly Father wants us to live.

*   *   *

CHAPTER TEN

*   *   *

THE MISSIONARY ADVENTURES OF
THE SONS OF MOSIAH

After Alma the 2nd rested for a while from his missionary efforts, he decided to make a journey to Manti. To his great surprise and delight, he met his good friends, the sons of Mosiah, on the road as they were headed to Zarahemla. They had been teaching successfully among the Lamanites for fourteen years. This reunion with Alma gave them a chance to fill him in on their many missionary adventures.

Shortly after they had arrived in the land of Nephi years earlier, the land having become the land of the Lamanites, Ammon the 2nd, the unspoken leader of the brothers, did bless each of them, and then each departed to their separate ways to preach the gospel to whomever they should encounter. (Alma 17:)

Whether by chance or divine design, Ammon ended up in the land of Ishmael, where the descendants of father Ishmael had settled. Ishmael was the father-in-law of Nephi the 1st and his brothers. He had died during the eight-year trek in the wilderness from old Jerusalem to the original Bountiful on the Arabian seacoast, the place where Nephi had built the ship for the long voyage to the

Americas. After hundreds of years, Ishmael's posterity had gradually deteriorated in their original faith to become Lamanites in deeds, attitude, and culture.

Upon arriving in this land of Ishmael, Ammon the 2nd was immediately bound and taken before the King, Lamoni, a descendant of Ishmael, but who was now considered to be a Lamanite King.

This particular incident is often confused with another very similar incident wherein thirty years earlier, in the early days of King Mosiah, another young man also named Ammon, who was Ammon the 1st the Mulekite from Zarahemla, led his men to the land of Nephi were they were taken and bound before a King called Limhi. Limhi was a nominal Nephite King under the rule of the Lamanites and he and his people were still subject to the whims of the ruling Lamanite King. This King Limhi just happened to be the son of the nefarious and infamous wicked King Noah, but he was certainly much less controversial and for the most part a just man. That particular incident with Ammon the 1st resulted in the deliverance of King Limhi's people from the rule of the Lamanites with the help of the Lord. The King Limhi episode concluded with a joyous uniting of Limhi's people with the people of Zarahemla at which point they were assimilated into the kingdom of King Mosiah the 2nd. (Mosiah 7:6-14) Now thirty years later, we have a different Ammon, Ammon the 2nd that is now standing before the Lamanite King Lamoni.

This particular Lamanite King, Lamoni, pointedly asks Ammon the 2nd the missionary son of Mosiah, if he wishes to dwell among the Lamanites. Ammon answers yes, maybe even for the rest of his life. Lamoni is so impressed with Ammon that he not only commands that his bands be loosened, but even offers him one of his own daughters for a wife. Ammon politely declines the gift of a princess wife, and says his only desire is to serve the King. King Lamoni respects his wishes and abides by sending him to watch over the King's flocks along with the king's other servants.

Three days later at the waters of Sebus, Ammon and the other servants are herding the King's flocks to water when Lamanite ruffians and thieves scatter the flocks and their herders. This was their unscrupulous habit in order to gather up the strays to add to their own herds. Lamoni's servants were now beside themselves in fear, because King Lamoni had a reputation for severely punishing, even slaying his servants who lose his flocks. Ammon saw this as an opportunity to impress and gain the trust of his fellow servants so that they might listen to his words of faith later. He then encouraged them to gather up the flocks and be of good cheer. No sooner had they done this, than the ruffians returned. Ammon told the servants to gather around the flocks and protect them, while he himself would contend with these unscrupulous and be-deviling ruffians.

The thieves almost laughed when they saw Ammon, a lone man, coming to stop them. They soon took him quite seriously, though, when he began to knock them to the ground with his deadly sling and some very hard rocks. Absolutely incensed with anger, they tried to kill him. After failing to hit him with any of their rocks, they attacked him with clubs, which they soon found out wasn't a good idea, either. Ammon not only slew their brazen and fierce leader with his sword, but he also cut off the arms of six more of the surprised and utterly shocked thieves. These ruffians had had more than enough of Ammon.

The flocks were then watered and returned to the King's pasture, and the astonished servants, still being in awe, carried the severed arms to King Lamoni as proof of the unbelievable deed that Ammon had performed in behalf of their King. Lamoni was astonished at the testimony of Ammon's deeds, and speculated that he might even be the Great Spirit. He then asked, "Where is he now?" The servants replied that he was taking care of the King's horses. King Lamoni was even more amazed, so much so that he did not dare command that Ammon should come unto him.

Ammon finished his chores and then went into the King and asked what the King now desired of him. King Lamoni did not answer for an hour, and even then, only after Ammon was able to perceive his thoughts. Ammon stated the king's thoughts aloud, which astonished the King even more. Ammon convinced Lamoni that he himself was not the Great Spirit, but only his servant and that any power that he might have came from the Lord. Ammon then rehearsed the creation of the earth, the history of the prophets, and the history of his own ancestors from the time of Lehi's landing in the Americas, as well as the plan of redemption and the coming of Christ. King Lamoni was so touched by the spirit of truth that he fell to the ground and became as if he was dead. His servants then carried him to his wife and family, who perceived him to be deceased and went into a state of mourning. (Alma 18:)

Two days later, the family was preparing to bury King Lamoni, but the Queen having heard of Ammon the 2nd's "great powers" decided to call for him to come and see her husband, as one last desperate hope. Ammon complied with her request, looked at the King and said, "He is not dead, but he sleepeth in God, and on the morrow he shall rise again; therefore bury him not." (Alma 19:8) Ammon then asked the Queen if she truly believed that her husband would arise and she said she did.

The next day her husband the King arose, stretched out his hand to his Queen and testified of Christ saying, "I have seen my Redeemer." The spirit was so strong, that the King, the Queen, and even Ammon after thanking God, all fell to the earth. The servants who witnessed the miracles of Ammon also fell to the ground unconscious, all except a Lamanitish women, called Abish who had previously been converted years before when her father had had a remarkable vision. She then ran from house to house spreading the word, as a multitude of people began to gather and debated why the King's entire household was all dead.

One man in the crowd, who's brother had been slain by Ammon, when Ammon had protected the flocks of the King at the waters of Sebus, tried to strike the prostrate Ammon with his sword out of revenge, but he instantly fell dead, as the Lord fulfilled his promise to King Mosiah the 2nd that his sons would be protected on their missions.

This put a great fear into the multitude. Some declared that Ammon was the Great Spirit, while others argued that he was some kind of a monster, and "the contention began to be exceedingly sharp." Abish, the converted Lamanitish woman, upset by all the arguing, walked over to the unconscious Queen in tears, lifted up her hand, and to the great shock of all, helped the Queen to her feet. The Queen, after a short declaration of thanks to God, walked over to her husband the king, took him by the hand and helped him to his feet. The king rebuked the arguing people, and gave them a sermon regarding the words of Ammon. Amazingly many of them did believe and were converted. However there were many others who were skeptical and faithless unbelievers. They ignored the miracles and the truth and went about their business.

Meanwhile, Ammon and the king's servants arose and bore their testimonies to all that would listen. Many of the people in the multitudes believed the testimonies, were baptized, and a church was established among the Lamanites fulfilling Ammon's dream, and also the word of the Lord to Ammon's father, Mosiah; ". . . for many shall believe on their words."

See (Mosiah 28:7) (Alma chapter 19)

King Lamoni was so pleased with Ammon, that he very much wanted his own father, the King of all the land, to meet Ammon in person. Ammon however, received inspiration that it was not only a bad idea, but also that there were other pressing matters in the land of Middoni, namely the fate of his own brother. His brother, Aaron, and his companions were imprisoned in Middoni, and Ammon felt a great urgency to go and deliver them. King Lamoni said that was fine with him, but he wanted to go along with Ammon because the King in Middoni was a friend of his, and that might be of some help to Ammon.

As Ammon and King Lamoni were proceeding on their journey to Middoni, they unexpectedly ran into Lamoni's father, the King of all the land coming from the land of Nephi. Lamoni's father was upset that Lamoni had not attended the great feast that he had prepared for his sons, and was even less happy with the fact that his own son was traveling with a cunning and lying Nephite. Lamoni tried to explain, but his father commanded him to slay his new Nephite friend. Lamoni refused, and his father then drew his sword to strike his own son down. Ammon stepped forth to defend Lamoni, causing the father to turn and attempt to slay Ammon. In self-defense, Ammon withdrew his own sword, withstood the blows of the angry king and struck the king's arm with his deadly sharp sword disabling this very frightened King of all the land The King, suddenly becoming quite humble, begged for his life and offered Ammon what ever he desired in return for letting him live. Somewhat as a surprise to the King, Ammon simply asked for nothing more than the release of his brother Aaron and his brother's companions, and one other thing;

that the King should let his own son Lamoni retain his kingdom and be left free to make his own decisions without interference. The King of the land was so impressed with Ammon and his true concern and friendship for Lamoni that he not only granted all requests, but also invited Ammon and his brothers to come to his own kingdom as honored guests. He was very much interested in hearing the words of their ministry, after they had returned from their quest in the land of Middoni.

Ammon and Lamoni then proceeded on their journey to Middoni, where they found favor with the King of that land. Though Ammon's brother, Aaron, and his companions were hungry, thirsty, naked and abused, Ammon and Lamoni successfully obtained their release and the missionaries were finally delivered from their awful prison. (Alma 20:)

*   *   *

How did Aaron the brother of Ammon, and his companions end up in that prison? Fourteen years earlier, when the four sons of Mosiah, that is Ammon, Aaron, Himni, and Omner, had gone their separate ways to convert the Lamanites, Aaron went to the great city of Jerusalem on the borders of Mormon. The city was, of course, named after Father Lehi's original home across the great waters. Aaron found the New Jerusalem to be not only inhabited by Lamanites, but also by the hardened apostate Amalekites, and the wicked people of Amulon. The Amalekites were Nephite apostates who followed the order of Nehors, while the people of Amulon were the followers of King Noah's wicked priests and their wicked leader, a man called Amulon. The whole disgusting bunch were now all living together with the Lamanites in the great city of Jerusalem on borders of Mormon. The Lamanites were hard hearted, but these apostate Nephites were granite hard in their opposition and anger towards the Nephite people, and very dedicated to their own wicked ways. They truly had a deep hatred towards the Nephites, which penetrated to the marrow of their very bones.

Aaron began his preaching to the Amalekites in their own synagogues. They mocked him and argued with him until he finally saw the futility of getting them to listen, and so he left and headed for a village called Ani-anti. There he met two Nephite missionaries, Muloki and Ammah, who were also doing missionary work in the area. After another futile attempt at getting the hardhearted people to listen, the three of them left the village and journeyed to Middoni. Once again they encountered hardhearted people, only this time they were bound, abused, and cast into an awful prison, which is where Ammon and king Lamoni came to their rescue, negotiated successfully, and delivered them from their imprisonment.

Amazingly undaunted after all this, and even after their bad experiences in the abusive prison, they still continued to preach to the Lamanites. This time they were blessed by the Lord and actually had some success and brought many Lamanites to the "knowledge of the truth."

Meanwhile Ammon and king Lamoni returned to Lamoni's home, the land of Ishmael, to build synagogues and organize the teaching of Lamoni's people. Much to Ammon and king Lamoni's joy, they found that Lamoni's people "were zealous for keeping the commandments of God." (Alma 21: 23)

While Ammon was busy teaching the people of King Lamoni and establishing a church in that land, his brother Aaron and his missionary companions decided to visit Lamoni's father, the King of all the land who was residing in the land of Nephi, as they desired to take him up on his earlier invitation.

On their arrival, the King inquired as to why Ammon had not come with them, as he was still somewhat anxious to see Ammon again and wanted to ask him some questions regarding his religious beliefs. He was more or less satisfied with the explanation of why Ammon wasn't able to come, and then the inquisitive King revealed to Aaron that he had been troubled by "the greatness of the words of thy brother Ammon", and he now desired that Aaron and his companions should administer to him.

Aaron proceeded and did firstly establish that God was the same as "The Great Spirit" which the King believed had created all things. Then expounding upon the fall of Adam, he proceeded with the plan of redemption prepared from the foundation of the world, and concluded with the atonement of Christ breaking the bands of death. With these words, Aaron was able touch the King's heart with truth and a special spirit that the King could feel, a spirit, which seemed to envelope the King's whole soul. The King fell to the earth and beseeched God to make Himself known, wherein he was struck as if he were dead. This very scenario between Aaron and Lamoni's father is very similar to the earlier situation where Ammon the 2nd had converted King Lamoni, himself.

Meanwhile, the servants ran to the Queen with the news, who then returned to find Aaron and his brothers standing over the body of Lamoni's father, the King of all the land. In anger, the Queen ordered the servants to slay Aaron and his companions thinking that they had done harm to the King, but the servants having witnessed the miraculous event, were afraid to even touch Aaron. Perceiving the fear of the servants, the frightened Queen called instead for the people, themselves, to come and slay the Nephite missionaries.

In order to avoid an increasingly tense and troublesome situation, Aaron walked over to the King, touched his hand and helped him to his feet. The great King of the Land then ministered to his wife and even to his servants, and amazingly his entire household was converted to the Lord. After attempting to appease the murmuring of the multitude, the King caused that Aaron and his brethren should begin to teach the somewhat rowdy crowd. He also caused that a proclamation should be sent through out the land, that no one should touch or harm in anyway Aaron and his companions as they went about their business, the business of teaching the people of the land the word of God. (Alma 22:)

*   *   *

Alma chapter 22 also contains some interesting geographical notes. "And now it was only the distance of a day and a half's journey for a Nephite, on the line Bountiful and the land Desolation, from the east to the west sea; and thus the land of Nephi and the land of Zarahemla were nearly surrounded by water, there being a small neck of land between the land northward and the land southward." (Alma 22:32)

Some Book of Mormon readers conclude that this scripture means that Zarahemla and the city of Nephi were both located within the "narrow neck of land" being that they were both nearly surrounded by water, however most map makers conclude from Alma 22:27 that the land of Zarahemla and the land of Nephi were both south of the "narrow neck of land" but that the two areas were separated by a "narrow strip of wilderness" where Zarahemla was to the north of the wilderness strip, while the land of Nephi and the land of Lehi were below and to the south of the "narrow strip of wilderness."

*   *   *

"Book of Mormon lands were longer from north to south than from east to west. They consisted of two landmasses connected by an isthmus ("a narrow neck of land") flanked by an "east sea" and a "west sea" (Alma 22:27, 32). The land north of the narrow neck was known as the "land northward" and that to the south as the "land southward" (Alma 22:32).

The land southward was divided by a "narrow strip of wilderness" that ran from the "sea east" to the "sea west" (Alma 22:27). Nephites occupied the land to the north of this wilderness, and the Lamanites, that to the south. Sidon, the only river mentioned by name, ran northward between eastern and western wildernesses from headwaters in the narrow strip of wilderness (Alma 22:29). The Sidon probably emptied into the east sea based on the description of the east wilderness as a rather wide, coastal zone but its mouth is nowhere specified."—Encyclopedia of Mormonism, Vol.1, BOOK OF MORMON GEOGRAPHY

*   *   *

As Ammon, Aaron, and their brethren preached through out the lands that were to the south of the "narrow strip of wilderness", they began to have great success, converting literally thousands of the Lamanites, and their converts were described as those who "never did fall away." The brothers consecrated priest and teachers, and established churches in seven large areas among the Lamanites. The seven areas were the lands of Ishmael, Middoni, Shilom, and Shemlon, as well as three cities, Nephi, Lemuel, and Shimnilom.

These newly converted Lamanites not only committed themselves to the Lord, but also made an oath to never ever kill again and so they did lay down their weapons of war and made a sacred vow. Then in order to distinguish themselves from their unrepentant brethren, they changed the name by which they should be called from Lamanites to Anti-Nephi-Lehies. Later they would be known as the people of Ammon, or Ammonites.

The odd name of Anti-Nephi-Lehies appears to be somewhat contradictory, that is, if we interpret it in the usual way where anti means against or in opposition to. Although no Book of Mormon explanation has been given for it, some people speculate that it simply means, being the opposite of the people who lived in the lands of Nephi-Lehi at that time, while other scholars say that the Hebrew word for anti means "a reflection of" or in this case, to be a reflection of Nephi and Lehi, and that these people wanted to try to emulate these respected prophets.

Meanwhile, the Amalekites and Amulonites, being hard hearted Nephite apostates, not only did not convert, but became even a more hard hearted people, stirring up the unconverted Lamanites to a great hatred towards the Anti-Nephi-Lehies or the people of Ammon. The wicked apostate Nephites finally convinced the unconverted Lamanites to revolt against their own king, who was the repentant and the newly converted old Lamanite King of all the land. Meanwhile they prepared to take up arms to destroy the Anti-Nephi-Lehies.

Before the old Lamanite King of the land died, he conferred his kingdom upon his own son, who was the brother of King Lamoni, "and he called his name Anti-Nephi-Lehi." The old King then passed away while the more wicked Lamanites continued to prepare for war against the Anti-Nephi-Lehies. (Alma 24:3)

Being aware of these dangerous events, Ammon and his brethren held a council with Lamoni and his brother, Anti-Nephi-Lehi, who was now the new King. They debated on what they should do about the pending attack of the Lamanites and their hateful allies, those hateful Nephite apostates. The Anti-Nephi-Lehies and their new King not only absolutely refused to fight, but made a point of total commitment against killing of any kind, and they backed up this oath by burying their weapons of war in the ground to show their true feelings to never kill again. Some people have speculated that this very act was possibly the beginning of the American Indian tradition of "burying the hatchet" as a symbolic sign of peace.

Because the newly converted Lamanites had suffered much guilt and a painful repentance process for the previous killings they had committed, they said that they did not know if the Lord would forgive them a second time, and so they refused to take up weapons of any kind, not even to defend themselves, or their wives, or their children, choosing to die in the hands of the Lord rather than taking another life.

When the Lamanites finally did attack, the Anti-Nephi-Lehies went out and met them and did then lie down in front of their enemies, calling upon the name of the Lord, and submitting themselves to the mercy of their attackers. One thousand and five of them were slaughtered in the first attack. On seeing that their brethren were praising God even as they died in the slaughter, over a thousand of the wicked Lamanites repented of the evil massacre, and then joined the surviving peaceful Anti-Nephi-Lehies. Not particularly surprising, not a single Amalekite or Amulonite repented and so did continue in their evilness and their violent hateful ways. (Alma 24:)

Many of the unrepentant Lamanites decided to leave the Anti-Neph-Lehies alone, and instead, take out their revenge upon the Nephites. During the ensuing battles, hundreds of the vengeful Lamanites were slain, as were most of the descendants of Amulon, and even the wicked priests of King Noah, thus fulfilling the prophesies of Abinadi.

When the surviving Lamanites could see that they could not overpower the Nephites, many of them returned to the land of Ishmael and the land of Nephi and joined with Anti-Nephi-Lehies or the people of Ammon, buried their weapons, and were peacefully assimilated into the communities of the righteous people of God.

In seeing these great things happening, Ammon and his brothers rejoiced exceedingly, and Ammon began enumerating all the great fruits of their labors among the Lamanites, which had changed the lives of literally thousands. Aaron, half joking, rebuked him for boasting. Ammon replied that he knew that he, himself, was nothing, and that he boasted only on behalf of his God, and of his great power and mercy, and the mindfulness of all his children, whatever land they may be in.

The apostate Amalekites suffered huge losses at the hands of the Nephites, and when they saw that they could not defeat the Nephites, they decided to take out their revenge upon the defenseless Anti-Nephi-Lehies. Ammon the 2nd who became greatly concerned about their safety, implored the King of the Anti-Nephi-Lehis to return to Zarahemla with him and his brothers. King Anti-Nephi-Lehi was reluctant to go along with the suggestion, because he feared that the Nephite people would still be angry with his people due to their past aggressions as Lamanites, even though he and his humble and repentant followers were now willing to be slaves to the Nephites. Ammon said that he would inquire of the Lord. The Lord plainly told Ammon to get the Anti-Nephi-Lehies out of the land and lead them to safety, because Satan had a great hold upon the hearts of the Amalekites who were determined to completely destroy the Anti-Nephi-Lehis, or as they were now called, the people of Ammon.

So the Ant-Nephi-Lehies gathered up their flocks and herds and went with Ammon and his brothers north into the "narrow strip of wilderness" and on towards the land of Zarahemla. They camped on the borders of the land, while Ammon and his brothers went on into Zarahemla, where they ran in to Alma the 2nd for a most joyful reunion. They then all went before the chief judge and rehearsed their story of all the things that had taken place in the land of Nephi.

The chief judge sent a proclamation out among the people to see how they felt about the Anti-Nephi-Lehies living among them. The Nephite people were receptive, even offering the Anti-Nephi-Lehies a land of their own, which was called the land of Jershon, where they could be protected from the Lamanites and the Amalekites by their Nephite defenders. The Anti-Nephi-Lehies, who were now the people of Ammon, received the news with great joy. They were pleased that they were only asked to provide provisions for the Nephite army, in return for their safety and defense. The land that was given to them in Jershon was on the east seacoast, south of the land of Bountiful. The people of Ammon took possession of this land, and became "distinguished for their zeal towards God, and also towards men . . . and they were firm in the faith of Christ, even unto the end." Thus they were a highly favored people of the Lord, abhorring bloodshed, and they were extremely zealous in their faith. (Alma 27:)

*   *   *

CHAPTER ELEVEN

* * *

BACK IN ZARAHEMLA

In the fifteenth year of the reign of the judges, while guarding the borders of Jershon, the protective Nephite soldiers happened upon the Lamanite armies who were searching for the innocent people of Ammon in the wilderness. A colossal and very bloody battle took place resulting in a great many deaths among the Nephite soldiers. Yet there were far more deaths among the enemy as tens of thousands of the Lamanites were slaughtered, and the survivors were scattered and driven back into the wilderness. (Alma 28:)

For the time being, the Lamanites were successfully driven out of the lands of the Nephites and a period of peace followed settling upon the land for two years. Alma the 2nd and Ammon the 2nd and his brothers were overjoyed by their missionary successes and were very pleased that the people were now living righteously.

Unfortunately, the peaceful easy good life was to be short lived. Shangri-La on this earth exists only in the minds of men. In the real world, continued trials, hardships, challenges, and tests of faith are an ongoing part of our earthly lives, as we journey through mortality proving ourselves to be or to not be, faithful servants of God. So it was with the people in Zarahemla.

In the seventeenth year of the reign of judges, an Anti-Christ came into the land of Zarahemla. This evil one went by the name of Korihor. There was no law among the Nephites that prohibited a man from preaching whatever he desired. So this very unscrupulous character, with his self-promoting motives carefully hidden behind his smiling façade, began to preach that the people were foolish for believing in this mythical Christ and the foolish traditions of their fathers. He told them that they were just stupid to believe in some ridiculous mythical afterlife. He implied that there was no such thing as sin or even crime. He assured his listeners that the only true morality was that a man should prosper any way that he could, relying on his own genius and strength to further his lot in life and get what ever he could get any way he could get it. This worldly preaching and immoral philosophy along with his selfish ideas of how to live, very much appealed to the many greedy and immoral people among the Nephites. In turn they began to commit all manner of whoredoms while they appeased their most base appetites and their seemingly unquenchable lustful desires.

Thus having had great success and influence among many of the less righteous Nephites, Korihor decided to take his show on the road to the Land of Jershon. These people of Ammon, formerly known as the Ant-Nephi-Lehies, were not so foolish as some of the Nephites. They simply did not buy his flattering words, his false reasoning, and his ridiculous spiel, and they remained dedicated to God. Consequently they took hold of him, bound him, and carried him before their spiritual leader, Ammon the 2nd, son of Mosiah the 2nd, who was now a high priest over the land of Jershon. With Korihor standing before him, Ammon decreed that Korihor should be exiled. Certainly to some, this must have seemed like insufficient punishment for such heresy and such a vile human bean. Never the less, upon this turn of events, Korihor was released and left Jershon unharmed as he proceeded to new lands to spread his wicked ideas in the land of Gideon where he once again preached the flattering and tempting words of his heresy. Once again he was taken and bound by the local people.

This time he was taken before the high priest Giddonah, where the unrepentant Korihor argued that Giddonah and the other Nephite leaders were just using the people, and were deliberately keeping the people under some kind of religious bondage with their stupid, foolish, and long time traditional spiritual teachings.

When the high priest Giddonah and the local chief judge could see that Korihor was well beyond any normal reasoning and it was highly unlikely that he would ever change, they brought him before Alma the 2nd who was the chief priest of all the land, and subsequently taken before the chief judge who was also the governor of all the land. (Alma 30:29)

*   *   *

Encyclopedia of Mormonism, Vol.3, PRIEST, AARONIC PRIESTHOOD

"While most English-speaking Christian traditions use the word priest to refer both to the ancient Levitical roles and to the elders of the early Christian churches, who had responsibilities to preside over and instruct congregations, the two offices are separated in the LDS Church in that priests are of the Aaronic Priesthood and perform basic ordinances and otherwise assist the elders and high priests of the Melchizedek Priesthood.

Because there were no descendants of Aaron among the Nephites or Lamanites, priests in the Book of Mormon held the Melchizedek

Priesthood and thus engaged both in the sacrificial functions and in the broader presiding and teaching functions." (Alma 18:24; 45:22)

*   *   *

As Korihor stood before the chief priest and the chief judge, he brazenly accused them of glutting themselves upon the labors of the people, leading them astray, and promoting the false traditions and myths of their fathers for their own selfish gain. Alma's rebuttal was backed with testimony and truth as he put Korihor on the spot about denying God and Christ. Seemingly unaffected, Korihor said that he would believe in Alma's God only when he was actually shown a sign that God really does exist. Alma justifiably replied, "Thou hast had signs enough. Will ye tempt your God?" (Alma 30: 44) Alma then went on to say that he, himself, was grieved for Korihor because of the hardness of his heart, but it would be better for Korihor's soul to be lost than for many souls to be destroyed. Therefore, Alma pronounced that Korihor would be struck dumb if he denied God one more time. The foolish Korihor was unerringly stubborn and absolutely defiant and so consequently and justifiably, he was struck dumb resulting in being completely unable to speak. On seeing this, the chief judge passed Korihor a note asking if he believed in God now. Being dramatically humbled and frightened, Korihor wrote a note back saying that he knew that only God had the power to do this to him, and he now admitted that the devil had deceived him, and he beseeched Alma to take the curse from him. Alma said it was too late and the Lord's will would be done. (Alma 30: 55)

The word of Korihor's fate, spread through out the land as he went from house to house begging for food. Many of his frightened converts, on seeing and hearing of their fallen hero's disturbing and unhappy fate, conveniently found religion again and repented.

Korihor became a very miserable and wretched vagabond. As he went among the apostate Zoramites begging for his food, and as fate and justice would have it, he was trampled to death, "and thus we see that the devil will not support his children at the last day, but doth speedily drag them down to hell" in the end. (Alma 30: 60)

*   *   *

The apostate Zoramites who trampled upon Korihor's weakened body, were descendants of Zoram the 1st, the servant of Laban who followed Nephi the 1st to the Promised Land. In spite of their righteous heritage, some 500 years later they had become apostates without sympathy, caring, or faith, and now had no desire to be obedient to God. They were led once again by a man named Zoram, only this misguided Zoramite leader was now teaching them that they should bow down before dumb idols.

To put it mildly, "They did pervert the ways of the Lord" and built synagogues which contained a tall narrow stand or platform in the center, called Rameumptom. This is where they one at a time would climb up and stand upon the platform and then cry aloud thanking their Spirit God that they had not been so foolish as to believe in the traditions of the Nephites and the mythical Christ of the Nephites. While blatantly bragging that God had made it known to them "that there shall be no Christ", they also emphasized that they were God's "holy children" and they had been elected to be saved, while everyone around them would be cast down to hell. This they did once a week without fail, boasting and repeating the same prayer every time, and then totally ignoring God the rest of the week. Meanwhile they set their true hearts upon silver and gold and all manner of things of the world. They did also exhibit great pride in themselves and their accomplishments forgetting the very God who created them. (Alma 31:)

*   *   *

The strange name of Rameumptom, which was what the Zoramites called the tall stand that they prayed from, may seem to Book of Mormon critics like another storybook word from the Joseph Smith fairy tale. Interestingly enough, those same critics might be somewhat surprised to know that the Semitic root word "ram" means a high place in ancient Hebrew, just as it does today in the names of the Israeli towns of Rammallah and Rameem, both of which are located in high places on the hilltops in the modern state of Israel. It is highly unlikely that Joseph Smith would have known this very appropriate meaning for this Semitic prefix in the word Rameumptom. This is just one more piece of evidence supporting the authenticity of the Book of Mormon and strongly supporting the idea that Joseph could not have wrote this book strictly from his imagination.

*   *   *

Alma the 2nd, troubled by what he learned about the activities of the Zoramites took the sons of Mosiah and his own two sons with him to the Zoramite land called Antionum on the east seacoast, just south of the land of Jershon. He also took along his old missionary companion, Amulek, as well as the former wicked lawyer, Zeezrom, who was now reformed and repentant. Their goal was to reclaim the lost souls of the Zoramites.

On arrival, Alma prayed mightily to the Lord. Then with great faith, he laid his hands upon the heads of his faithful companions, and filled them with the spirit of missionary work. They all separated and then went forth without purse or script to teach among the poor, and they did happily have some success.

The poor had been cast out of the synagogues by the prideful and snooty priests because of their perceived filthiness, and so the poor felt despised of men and they simply felt that they had no place to worship. Alma the 2nd posed this question to them "..do you suppose that ye cannot worship God save it be in your synagogues only?" He then explained what faith was, and encouraged them to nourish the seeds of faith to grow into a most precious and sweet fruit of everlasting life. (Alma 32:)

He quoted the Old Testament prophet, Zenos, who taught that a person should pray and worship whether they were in the wilderness or in their fields, and to pray in all places. There was another prophet mentioned in the brass plates also spoken of by Alma. It was Zenock, who had taught that God's mercy is bestowed because of his beloved son. Unfortunately, these teachings from these two Old Testament prophets are missing from our present day Bible.

*   *   *

"Alma 33:16 contains the only direct quotation of Zenock's words, citing him as one of many Israelite prophets who foretold the mission of the Son of God (Alma 33:14-17; cf. 34:7) and quoting him on the mercies that God grants because of his Son. Alma2 noted, however, that because the people "would not understand" Zenock's words, they "stoned him to death" (Alma 33:17)" (See Zenock; Encyclopedia of Mormonism)

"It is also evident from the scriptural quotations in the Book of Mormon that the plates of brass contained a more extensive record of the writings of Hebrew prophets than does the present Old Testament. For example, the Book of Mormon includes prophecies of Joseph of Egypt that are not found in the Bible, as well as writings of Zenos, Zenock, Neum, and Ezias, prophets who are not specifically named in the Old Testament." (See Book of Mormon: Plates and Records; Encyclopedia of Mormonism)

*   *   *

Alma's old missionary companion, Amulek, also spoke and testified to the poor among the Zoramites "that Christ shall come among the children of men" taking upon himself the transgressions of his people and "atone for the sins of the world."

After Amulek spoke, Alma, and his fellow missionaries concluded their preaching among the Zoramites, and they did journey to Jershon to be with the people of Ammon.

Meanwhile, the wicked among the Zoramites, who's evil craft had now been exposed, went surreptitiously among the people to find out "privily" how the people felt about the words of Alma, Amulek, and their missionary brethren. Consequently, every one of the common people who said that they believed in the words of the missionaries was then cast out, and so a great many good people were forced to leave their homes and go to Jershon where they were ministered to by Alma and his brethren.

The wicked leaders among the Zoramites tried to intimidate the compassionate people of Ammon so that in fear they would kick out the refugees. The wicked Zoramites even threatened the faithful if they didn't do it. However, the courageous people of Ammon didn't yield, but actually took in the poor of the Zoramites feeding and clothing them. This provoked the wicked Zoramites to great anger, as they prepared for war and stirred up the Lamanites to join with them against the innocent people of Ammon.

In the eighteenth year of the reign of judges, the people of Ammon actually had to leave their land of Jershon for their own safety. Meanwhile the Nephite armies went to war against the Lamanites and Zoramites in defense of the innocent people of Ammon.

Due to the wars, bloodshed, rampant contention, and the great iniquity widespread among the people of the land, Alma's words were rejected. The people were offended by his warnings and admonishments, and their hearts did wax hard against the word of the Lord. Alma became discouraged and sorrowful and so "being grieved for the iniquity of his people", he had become somewhat disillusioned and consequently he had become greatly concerned for the welfare of his own sons.

So he gathered his three sons together to speak to them and give them wise counsel and appropriate warnings about the consequences of living like their peers and the rest of the people around them. Even if he had given up on trying to persuade his own incorrigible people, he at least had to try to save his own sons from the worldliness of a wayward society. (Alma 35:)

*   *   *

In Alma Chapters 36 through 42, Alma bares testimony to his three sons, Helaman, Shiblon, and Corianton. He gives them wise counsel individually; father to son, and his wise advice to them is recorded for us to peruse in Alma's own words in the book of Alma.

Speaking first to Helaman, he goes into some detail telling his oldest son of his own personal conversion, which came not by his own worthiness, but by God's need to get his attention as he tried to destroy the church of God. He tells Helaman nothing was as bitter as the anguish and pain of recognizing his own sins, and yet nothing quite as exquisite as cleansing his soul with the joy of truly repenting. Alma went on to say, that since his conversion, he had been bound, imprisoned, and had nearly suffered death at the hands of his enemies, but the Lord had always delivered him. His trust in the Lord was now unshakeable.

He went on to recount the deliverance of the Lord's chosen people from Egypt, and the deliverance of his own ancestors from the destruction at Jerusalem, as well as the deliverance of their own Nephite people from captivity and bondage by the Lamanites down to this very day. Finally, he reminded Helaman that as long as he kept the commandments he would prosper, but if "ye will not keep the commandments of God ye shall be cut off from his presence." He told Helaman to counsel with the Lord in all his doings, and finally he commanded his son, "that ye keep a record of this people."

Giving a much shorter version of this same counsel to his son Shiblon, he praised Shiblon's faithfulness in the face of being bound and stoned by the Zoramites and still having the patience and trust in the Lord that he would be delivered. Never the less, he warned Shiblon about pride, boasting in his own wisdom and strength, idleness, unbridled passions, and against vain prayers like those of the Zoramites. Then he told him to be sober and go teach the word.

Lastly he spoke to his son Corianton and chastised him for boasting in his own strength and wisdom, but even more grievous than that, for consorting with the harlot Isabel, saying that it was not only a "most abominable above all sins save it be the shedding of innocent blood or denying the Holy Ghost," but in the bad example that he set for others, he had dissuaded the Zoramites from listening to the word of God. He tells his young impetuous son, that you cannot hide your crimes from God. He also spoke of wisdom and moral and spiritual strength. He told Corianton to not to endeavor to excuse his self and his own sins in the least manner, as he explained the absolute need for justice as well as mercy, otherwise "God would cease to be God." He spoke of the resurrection and the fate of the righteous in the hereafter, as well as the fate of the souls of the wicked after they die. He then counsels Corianton to repent, and to especially stay close to his brothers, to counsel with them and to be nourished by his family. Finally, he told Corianton that "Ye are called of God to preach the word unto this people."

Then expounding upon the atonement of Christ, he encouraged all of his sons to serve their God and their fellowmen by bringing many souls to repentance.

(Alma Chap. 36 through Chap. 42)

Helaman, Shiblon, and Corianton were inspired by their father's words, and thus fed by this spiritual energy, they accompanied their father as they all went forth to declare the word and the truth of the gospel among the people "according to the spirit of prophecy and revelation; and they preached after the Holy Order of God by which they were called." (Alma 43:2)

*   *   *

CHAPTER TWELVE

* * *

CHIEF CAPTAIN MORONI

In the eighteenth year of the reign of the judges, "the Zoramites became Lamanites." They were led by a man called Zerahemnah, and they joined up with the Lamanites and they became a significant part of the leadership in the Lamanite army as they agreed to carry out their mutual desire to destroy the Nephites. Zarahemnah knew that the Amalekites, being apostate Nephites after the order of Nehor, were even more hateful and murderous towards the Nephites than either the Zoramites or Lamanites. In light of this, he appointed captains from among the Amalekites to be over all the armies that were going to battle against the opposition with orders to enslave or destroy the Nephite people. Being completely devoid of morality or compassion in his desire to destroy all of the Nephite people, he also wanted the peaceful people of Ammon to be eradicated too.

The combined Lamanite forces gathered in Antionum, the land of the Zoramites. This was located to the south of where the defenseless people of Ammon dwelled in the land of Jershon on the east coast. The Nephites were keenly aware of these movements and those menacing preparations that the opposition was making for war, and they were very much determined to defend the people of

Ammon, as well as their own wives, children, and families, not to mention the precious liberty of all Nephites.

There was only one man that they trusted to lead them against the tens of thousands of men in the combined murderous Lamanite armies. His name was Moroni, a young twenty five year old man of amazing courage, faith, and strength, not to mention an inspired military strategist. This Moroni the 1st was then appointed to be Chief Captain over all the Nephite armies. He not only prepared his armies with swords and all manner of weapons, but with breastplates, shields, protective headgear, and thick clothing. Because the Lamanite armies were basically naked except for the skins that girded their loins and the primitive weapons that they carried, they were very much intimidated by the Nephite armies and their armor. Therefore instead of attacking the Nephite armies face to face at the borders of Jershon, they instead went by stealth into the wilderness to circumvent the Nephites. During the execution of this strategy, they took over the southern lands of the Nephites called Manti, which was near the head of the river Sidon in the narrow strip of wilderness.

Being aware of this ominous situation, Captain Moroni sent messengers to the prophet, Alma the 2nd, to ask his help and to inquire of the Lord as to how they should defend themselves. He also deployed spies to watch the Lamanite camps and there in received valuable intelligence from them as well. So then, being well informed by all of his messengers and advisors, he was ready to make a decision.

He sent half his army to the land of Manti. There he deployed part of his men on the south east of the hill Riplah, and the other part on the west side, flanking both sides of the valley. One of Moroni's best and most loyal officers, the ever-faithful Lehi the 3rd, led the men on the south. Lehi attacked the Lamanites from the rear and drove them towards Captain Moroni. The plan worked and despite the Lamanite army being more than double that of the Nephites, as well as being highly motivated by the extreme hatred of the Amalekite captains, the Lamanite army soon found themselves encircled by the attacking Nephite army and trapped by the stratagem of Captain Moroni with no options for getting away. They were "struck with terror."

Captain Moroni, being much more than just a fierce and wise warrior, had compassion upon the trapped Lamanites and ordered his men to halt the attack. He then spoke to Zarahemnah saying that the Nephites did not desire the blood of the Lamanites nor did they have any desire to put them in bondage, but he did insist that all the Lamanites put down and surrender their arms. He also asked that they should make a vow to not come against the Nephites ever again.

Zarahemnah said that he would be willing to put down his arms, but that he would never swear an oath to not attack the Nephites again. This was simply beyond his own ideology, his personal hatred, and the deep resolve that he had to destroy the Nephites. Captain Moroni responded by saying that they would either swear the oath or they would not be allowed to leave alive. At this point, in a fit of anger, Zarahemnah rushed towards Moroni determined to kill him. One of Moroni's men immediately saw the danger for his commander, and struck Zarahemnah with his sword and thus sliced off part of his scalp. Then taking the scalp on the tip of his sword, the soldier paraded it in front of Zarahemnah's men saying that if they did not surrender and swear an oath of peace, they would all "fall to the earth." The gruesome display had the desired effect and so being struck with fear and afraid for their very lives, many of the Lamanites threw down their weapons and made a covenant of peace.

The other warriors were not inclined to give up so easily, as the newly scalped and very angry Zarahemnah was now stirring them into a rage. The bloody battle began again with the same hopeless results for the Lamanites. In the end, Zarahemnah saw the futility of fighting against the powerful and well-armored Nephites and finally did concede. He then, along with all his men, did promise to lay down their arms and swear a covenant of peace. The people of Nephi rejoiced once again in the deliverance from their enemies and gave thanks to their God. (Alma 44:)

*   *   *

In the nineteenth year of the reign of the judges, Alma the 2nd questioned his son Helaman the 2nd about his beliefs and his faith in Christ and his resolve to obey the commandments. Helaman responded by saying, "Yea, I will keep the commandments with all my heart." Alma then prophesied privately to his son that in 400 years from the time that Christ should appear, that the people of Nephi would dwindle in unbelief, and because of their iniquity, they would become extinct. He then blessed Helaman and his other sons, and pronounced a blessing upon the church, and all the faithful to follow. Upon this final note, Alma the 2nd departed out of the land of Zarahemla and "he was never heard of more; as to his death or burial we know not of." (Alma 45:18)

Following in their father's footsteps, Helaman the 2nd and his brethren "went forth to establish the church again in all the land" and they appointed priest and teachers over all the churches.

Unfortunately there was a large group of unscrupulous Nephites, many of them who were judges, who were "wroth" with Helaman and his preaching. A large and strong man named Amalickiah, who had a very ambitious goal to rid the community of Helaman and his brethren, had a strong desire to become the King. He was the leader of the rebels who desired a king. Many of the Nephite people, who now seemed very quick to forget how the Lord had delivered them from their enemies, were enticed by the flattering words of Amalickiah and were becoming more worldly and wicked by the day.

Captain Moroni, being disappointed in his people and angry with the rebel Amalickiah, tore off a piece of his coat and wrote upon it, "In memory of our God, our religion, and freedom, and our peace, our wives, and our children." He then fastened it to a pole and called it "the title of liberty" while he bowed himself before God and prayed "mightily" for the blessings of liberty and the "Christians" possessing the land. (Alma 46:13) Thus Captain Moroni was able to rally his people and they made a covenant "that they would not forsake the Lord their God" and that they would "support the cause of freedom."

When the evil Amalickiah saw that the people were turning against him, he took his followers and headed for the land of Nephi to the south of the "narrow strip of wilderness." There he was able to stir up the wicked Lamanites and add even more fuel to the fire of the hatred that they had for the Nephites.

The accommodating Lamanite King, in collusion with Amalickiah, ordered his people to take up arms against the Nephites, but the majority of the Lamanite soldiers were afraid to fight the Nephites. Never the less, the King gave authority to Amalickiah to be the new chief commander over his warriors, or at least the ones who weren't afraid to fight the Nephite army. They would be the very ones who would be obedient to the King and their new commander and do battle against the better-equipped Nephite enemy.

Meanwhile all those Lamanites, who had been reluctant to follow the King's orders and fight against the Nephite army, retreated to Mount Antipas under leadership of a Lamanite commander called Lehonti. Little did they know that they were going to be involved in the fight, one way or another.

The conniving Amalickiah had a cunning plan. After prolonged entreaty, he was able to persuade Lehonti to come down from the mountain and meet him in a secret meeting where they would make a very devious and private agreement. The basis of this secret plan was to have Lehonti's soldiers surround Amalickiah's men during the night in order to force them to surrender. In return for this, Amalickiah's reward would be to become the second in command over the newly formed larger and combined army.

However, the devious Amalickiah had personal plans that went far beyond that. Giving a secret and unofficial order to one of his servants, Amalickiah persuaded him to surreptitiously administer poison to the unsuspecting Lehonti by small degrees. This inevitably resulted in Lehonti's death, and of course, there would now have to be a new commander over the combined Lamanite army. Guess who?

The self-appointed new general, Amalickiah, then proceeded with his new command to the great city of Nephi to "honor" his titled superior, the Lamanite King. As the King came out to receive them, Amalickiah's men bowed down before him as was expected. Following protocol, the King stretched his hand out to raise them, and at that moment one of them rose up and stabbed the unsuspecting King in the heart. The King's frightened servants then ran away. Amalickiah put on a great show as to how the King's own servants, who had shown their guilt by running away, had assassinated him. He then even went to the extent of sending part of his army to ostensibly track them down. Continuing to carry out his evil plan, he went before the Queen with his men who falsely witnessed that the King's own servants had killed him, and she believed them and she was easily charmed by Amalickiah's deceiving tongue.

The unbelievably devious and wicked Amalickiah, through trickery, fraud, and murder, thus ended up gaining the Queen of the land as his new wife, the Lamanite armies at his command, and the entire Kingdom of the Lamanites at his feet and bidding. (Alma 47:) All of this was not enough to satisfy the greedy power hungry Amalickiah. His self-serving egotistic desires were to be Commander and King over all the people in all of the lands, and he was very determined that this ambitious plan should include all of the Nephites and all of their brethren to be under his rule.

The honorable and wise Captain Moroni was not about to let this happen. Not only did he prepare his people spiritually, but he also had them erect many forts that were protected by tall mounds of dirt, and then he had them fortify the Nephite cities by encircling them with stonewalls and great mounds of soil.

Amalickiah's armies began their march towards Zarahemla going by way of Ammonihah, the very city which the Lamanites had previously annihilated leaving the "Desolation of Nehors" behind them. The city had since been rebuilt by the Nephites and was now strongly fortified by Captain Moroni's men.

The Lamanite army was astonished when they saw the fortifications. So they disappointedly retreated to what they thought would be the weaker Nephite city of Noah. They were again astonished at the fortifications, where one of Moroni's chief officers, Lehi the 3rd, was in charge and he and his men well prepared to defend the city.

This time the Zoramite officers decided that they weren't going to be deterred again. In the light of their own foolish pride and bravado, they felt compelled to attack the city. This foolish decision and their strategic stupidity resulted in more than a thousand of the Lamanite warriors being slaughtered as well as all of their chief captains being killed. On the other hand, not a single Nephite was slain.

The rest of the Lamanites fled. The egocentric Amalickiah was "exceedingly wroth" when he heard the news of the great Lamanite defeat at the hands of the Nephites, and in his great anger with venom dripping from his mouth and soul, he cursed God and swore an oath to drink the blood of Captain Moroni. (Alma 49:)

Meanwhile, Moroni was very aware that Amalickiah was not about to give up his obsession to enslave the Nephites, so he continued to fortify all Nephite cities with mounds of dirt topped by heavy timbers and sharp pickets. He also had his men patrol and fortify all the land between the east sea and the west sea on a line north of the "narrow strip of wilderness" just north of the headwaters of the river Sidon. The Lamanites were virtually cut off from the land of Zarahemla and all the lands Northward. At the south of the Nephite lands by the east sea, the Nephites built a city overlooking the land possessed by the Lamanites, which they called the city of Moroni. Between the city of Moroni on the east sea, and the city of Aaron, they built another city called Nephihah, thus creating a line of defense along their southern borders.

In the twenty first year of the reign of judges, the Nephites found themselves to be prosperous in their daily endeavors, a strong people in their militarily might, faithful and happy in their religion, and "..there never was a happier time among the people of Nephi, since the days of Nephi, than in the days of Moroni . . ." (Alma 50:23)

This time of peace continued for three years, until the twenty-fourth year of the reign of judges, when a civil dispute over the land between the Nephite land of Morianton and the Nephite land of Lehi ended up with the people of Morianton taking up arms against their own brethren. Out of fear, the people of Lehi fled to Captain Moroni for refuge. Morianton and his followers were afraid of what Moroni might do about this situation and so they fled northward towards the land of Desolation.

Captain Moroni sent a small army to stop them, an army led by one of his best officers, Teancum. The foolish Morianton and his followers decided to do battle against Teancum's army, which of course, was not a good idea. They were soundly defeated, which ultimately resulted in the death of their stubborn and rebellious leader. Morianton was killed by the sword of Teancum, and his now humbled people succumbed and were then returned to their own land where a peaceful agreement was made with the people of Lehi.

In this same year, Nephihah, the righteous chief judge of all the Nephites, died, wherein his son, Pahoran, was appointed in his stead. (Alma 50:)

Although Pahoran was a good man and tried to judge fairly, there was a contingent of the people called the king-men, who tried to demand that Pahoran should change the law so that the people could once again have a king to rule over them. Pahoran, of course, would not comply, and so these king-men decided that he should "be dethroned from the Judgment-seat."

The contention between the king-men and the supporters of Pahoran, who were called the Freemen, grew into a nasty feud, and finally had to be decided by the voice of the people. The majority voted for freedom and to give their support to Pahoran, their chief judge. The king-men were temporarily silenced, but certainly not dissuaded in their beliefs nor were they satisfied.

When the new leader of the Lamanite armies, the evil Amalickiah, made a choice to carry out his oath to drink the blood of Moroni, he once again became maliciously arrogant, full of false confidence, and stupid enough to attack Moroni and his Nephite army.

On hearing about the impending Lamanite attack, the king-men out of spite refused to fight the Lamanites, even to protect their own lands. Captain Moroni was so angered with them, that he sought and got the legal power to compel them to defend their country or be executed. Four thousand of the dissenters refused to comply and were executed by the sword. The rest of the king-men dissenters decided it was better to take their chances defending their country against the Lamanites than to die for certainty by the sword of Captain Moroni and his men.

The evil Amalickiah took advantage of Captain Moroni's distraction with the king-men, and was able to capture with his numberless host the city of Moroni, and six more Nephite cities, all of which gave the Lamanite army several fortified strongholds.

One of Moroni's military leaders and a skilled officer, Teancum, with an especially highly trained army, stopped Amalickiah's advancement towards the borders of the land of Bountiful and slew many of the Lamanites.

That night when both armies were camped, both sides were completely fatigued and so they were resting up for the battle to begin again on the morrow. While his men slept, Teancum sneaked into the tent of the evil Amalickiah, and he did thrust a javelin through his black heart, and thus he put a permanent end to the evil ways and the treachery of the infamous Amalickiah. (Alma 51:)

When the Lamanite army woke to find their leader assassinated, and saw that Teancum's army was more than ready to do battle, the Lamanites hastily retreated to the captured and fortified city of Mulek on the east seashore, south of Bountiful. Teancum wisely restrained himself and kept his distance from the enormous numbers of the Lamanite army while he waited on Captain Moroni. Moroni sent word to Teancum to retain the prisoners for exchange or ransom, and also to secure the narrow passage that led to the lands northward on the borders of Bountiful.

Unfortunately, the Lamanites were not without a leader for very long as Amalickiah's wicked brother, Ammoron, was soon appointed to reign in his stead. Ammoron, gathering a large army prepared to attack Moroni's army on the borders by the west sea, while the other part of his army harassed the Nephites on east seashores, putting the lives and liberty of all the Nephites in jeopardy.

Captain Moroni secured the southwest borders with many men, and then took part of his army to the east to reinforce Teancum. The Lamanites army had been reasonably safe from the Nephites as long as they stayed inside the captured and fortified cities, but Captain Moroni was not stupid nor without plans or a strategy.

He told Teancum to take a small band of men and bait the enemy by marching with his men down on the seashore in front of the Lamanites near the city of Mulek. The Lamanite army fell for it, and chased after Teancum's small band thinking that they would easily overcome him and rid themselves of a minor but bedeviling nuisance.

Their mistake was in leaving only a small contingency of men to protect the city. Captain Moroni's stratagem worked and his men soon had possession of the city of Mulek. Meanwhile Teancum and his men were leading the Lamanites towards the city of Bountiful where Moroni's other chief officer, Lehi the 3rd, was waiting with his army. When the Lamanites saw what was waiting for them, they retreated in confusion and hastily made their way back to what they thought was the safety of the city of Mulek. With Lehi's army to their rear and Moroni's army coming straight at them, the Lamanite warriors were caught between the hammer and the anvil.

Their leader was a Zoramite, called Jacob, and he inspired his men to fight with great fury in spite of their predicament. Many on both sides were killed or wounded. Even Captain Moroni was wounded, and Jacob the Zoramite commander was killed. What was left of the Lamanite army laid their weapons down at the feet of Moroni, and the prisoners were forced to bury the dead of both armies. The Lamanite prisoners were then marched to the land of Bountiful. (Alma 52:)

Captain Moroni left the city of Mulek under the command of his trusted friend and chief officer, Lehi the 3rd. Meanwhile, his other trusted commander, Teancum, was ordered to march the prisoners to the city of Bountiful where they were to dig a deep ditch around the city. They were to use the dirt to build a high mound on the inner banks, and then top it off with a wall of strong timbers. This became a very strongly fortified city and a very useful place to keep Lamanite prisoners incarcerated. It was virtually an impregnable prison built by the labor of the prisoner's own hands, leaving the Nephite soldiers free for other duties.

Back on the west sea, in the south, the Nephite army began to fight among themselves, and due to their own iniquity, lost some of their Nephite cities to the Lamanites.

The people of Ammon, formerly the Anti-Nephi-Lehis, had sworn an oath to not take up arms against any man, but now in seeing the dire circumstances that their Nephite brothers were placed in while protecting them, they felt compelled to break their oath in order to help the desperate cause. Helaman the 2nd, walking in the steps of his righteous father, Alma the 2nd, could not bear to see them break their sacred oath, and with some reasoning and spiritual conviction was able to convince them to not do it. After all, there was an unpleasant but never the less valid alternative.

The young men of the people of Ammon had not taken the sacred oath that their fathers had, and so these young men now desired to covenant to fight for the liberty of their families and for their Nephites brothers under the leadership of Helaman the 2nd. They were two thousand strong. They were dedicated and faithful young men who were well taught in righteousness by their mothers and were very ready to fight for God and country. So Helaman took command of them and marched them into battle against the Lamanites on the west sea in the southlands of the Nephites. They became known as the "two thousand stripling soldiers" or Helaman's stripling warriors. (Alma 53:22)

Meanwhile, the wicked Ammoron sent a messenger with a letter to Captain Moroni saying that he wished to exchange prisoners. Moroni replied with a proposal asking for one hostage Nephite family for each Lamanite warrior. He also demanded an agreement of a total withdrawal from the lands of the Nephites; either that, or the Nephites would totally commit to seeking the destruction of Ammoron and his army.

Ammoron fired back an angry message accusing Moroni of murdering his brother and taking away the Lamanite's rightful inheritance to govern all the land and all the people, including their lesser brethren, the Nephite people. He then defiantly denied the God of the Nephites, but in conclusion said that he would exchange prisoners anyway, even though he fully intended to continue the war. Moroni, of course, was angered and flatly refused.

Captain Moroni then came up with another plan and he sought out a Lamanite defector among his men. This man was a reformed Lamanite soldier who's Lamanite King had been murdered by the evil Amalickiah, and therefore he being angered by that incident now had defected and had become loyal to Captain Moroni. This Lamanite man, called by the very traditional name of Laman, agreed to Moroni's suggestion to go among the Lamanite guards in the city of Gid where the Nephite prisoners were being held and give unto them much wine. This he did, and when the Lamanites were good and drunk, Laman reported back to Moroni concerning their very inebriated condition. Moroni marched his men to Gid where they quietly stepped around and over the drunken guards and thus armed the prisoners within the walls to wait for the signal. Then Moroni and his men surrounded the city. The drunken Lamanite guards woke to find themselves hopelessly surrounded, inside and out, and so with no healthy alternative, they did surrender. Captain Moroni proceeded to have the Lamanite prisoners to labor in fortifying the city of Gid for the Nephites, and he then marched them to Bountiful to be imprisoned. (Alma 55:)

Meanwhile, Helaman wanting to keep his commander informed, sent Captain Moroni a letter updating Moroni in regards to the war in the quarter where he and his 2000 stripling warriors were fighting. He told Moroni that the Lamanites had taken many cities and that the armies of the Nephite commander, Captain Antipus, had become discouraged and weakened in spirit and body. Never the less, Helaman's young warriors had brought some hope to the bedraggled Nephite soldiers.

Helaman used his little army to draw out the Lamanites and lead them on a wild goose chase, while the Nephite Commander Antipus, pursued the Lamanites from behind. When the Lamanites turned to fight Antipus, Helaman's young stripling warriors attacked from the rear and fought like lions. Helaman said of his 2000 striplings; "never had I seen so great courage" as they fought with the strength of God.

The Lamanites surrendered under the onslaught, and not a single one of Helaman's 2000 young warriors was killed. Next, Captain Helaman led his young men towards the city of Manti to assist Moroni's other officers, Gid and Teomner, in retaking that city. Once again, the young warriors were used as bait to lead away the Lamanite army. Now left only lightly guarded by the Lamanite soldiers, the city of Manti was taken by the Nephites warriors without the shedding of a drop of blood. The Lamanite army, on return from their wild goose chase, saw that the Nephites had re-taken the city of Manti, and so did then flee into the wilderness, and the displaced Nephite families were returned to their homes, except the few who were carried off by the Lamanites. (Alma 58:)

Captain Moroni was very pleased with Helaman's success in recapturing the lands that had been lost and he caused his people to rejoice over this very good news. He then wrote a letter to Chief Judge Pahoran to secure the badly needed forces to help maintain those lands.

Meanwhile, the wicked Ammoron sent hordes of soldiers to attack the city of Nephihah, slaying many in a great slaughter and causing the Nephites to abandon it. Captain Moroni was very sorrowful about this turn of events, but not just because of the lost of Nephihah, but more so because of the wickedness of his own people and the seemingly indifference of their own Nephite government. (Alma 59:)

Moroni sent a second letter to Governor Pahoran desiring to know why he had not sent reinforcements and supplies to the Nephite soldiers on the front lines. He criticized Pahoran and the government for their neglect while the enemy slaughtered thousands of Nephites, even women and children. He told Pahoran, he was jeopardizing the very liberty of the Nephite people. Moroni concluded his epistle by actually threatening Pahoran and the government. He wrote that if Pahoran did not immediately send men and provisions that he, himself, would come to Zarahemla, and then in surprisingly strong language he went on to warn Pahoran, "and smite you with the sword, insomuch that ye can have no more power to impede the progress of this people in the cause of our freedom." (Alma 60:30)

Chief Governor Pahoran was grieved in his soul upon receiving the letter from the obviously angered and disgruntled Chief Captain Moroni, but he understood Captain Moroni's anger and frustration and knew that Moroni was not aware of all that had happened in the homeland. He replied to Moroni's letter and explained that he was not able to help Moroni's armies due to the insurrectionist among his own Nephite people who sought to take away the judgment seat from him. They had led away the hearts of many and had daunted the Freemen and the provisions that would have been sent to Moroni. Finally they had driven him, the very governor of the land, out of Zarahemla, along with his supporters to the land of Gideon. Meanwhile, the king-men under their new leader Pachus, had completely taken over the city of Zarahemla, had appointed a new king, and had made an alliance with the invading Lamanites.

The exiled Governor Pahoran then sent out a proclamation to gather free men everywhere to fight against the insurrection of the King-men. He also beseeched Captain Moroni to bring part of his army and to aid him and the rest of the free men to retake Zarahemla.

He closed his letter by encouraging Moroni to encourage Teancum and Lehi in their fight for liberty and to be strengthened in the Lord, and then ended his letter by sincerely calling Moroni his beloved brother. (Alma 61:)

Captain Moroni received Governor Pahoran's letter with mixed feelings. On the one hand, he was very happy to see that Pahoran was not deliberately neglecting the army's needs, and that he was certainly not a traitor to the cause of freedom, but on the other hand he was extremely disappointed and discouraged to hear of the fallen state of the Nephite people and the shocking and deteriorating circumstances in the great city of Zarahemla.

Complying with Pahoran's request, Moroni left the main army in the competent hands of his commanders, Teancum and Lehi, while he took a small army and headed towards the land of Gideon where Pahoran and his men were in refuge. On the way, he rallied as many men as he could to join him under the title of liberty to defend their freedom. Thousands of men responded to the rallying cry and proceeded to march to Gideon and join forces with Governor Pahoran to confront face to face the king-men now led by this new King, Pachus. The ensuing battle was swift and decisive, leaving the king-men imprisoned, their leader Pachus dead, and Governor Pahoran back in his judgment seat.

For the preservation of their very freedom, the laws of the land had necessarily become very strict, and the men of Pachus and all the king-men who refused to fight for their country, were promptly executed according to the laws that had previously been passed. And thus in the thirtieth year of the reign of judges, Captain Moroni and Governor Pahoran had once again restored a righteous leadership among the people, and peace once again fell upon the land of Zarahemla.

Within the next year, Captain Moroni sent six thousand men and provisions to the aid of commander Helaman, and another six thousand to his chief officers, Teancum and Lehi. Then Moroni with his own army, headed towards the captured city of Nephihah. While the Lamanites were asleep, Moroni and his men carefully scaled the walls and let themselves down inside the city and took it without losing a man. The Lamanite prisoners, seeing the futility of their cause, surprisingly asked to join the people of Ammon where they then became farmers and herdsmen relieving a great burden upon Moroni's armies.

Meanwhile, Captain Moroni and his men pursued the surviving Lamanite armies from city to city, until they had them all gathered in one big army on the east seashore of the land of Moroni. This is where their wicked King Ammoron, had led them to watch and wait for the next battle. The Nephite army surrounded the Lamanites here, and then rested up for the great battle to come.

Moroni's chief officer, commander Teancum, specifically blamed the wicked King Ammoron and his brother for all of the thousands of dead, and for a long bloody and unnecessary evil war. In his great anger, he contemplated and then carried out a plan where he did by stealth, slipped into the Lamanite camp and did put a javelin through the heart of the evil King Ammoron, just the way he had Ammoron's brother, the wicked Amalickiah. Unfortunately, this time the servants were awakened by the King's cries, and commander Teancum was hunted down and killed by them.

Captain Moroni and his other chief officer, commander Lehi, were heartbroken when they heard the news concerning commander Teancum's untimely death, and they did greatly lament over the great loss of such an excellent military officer and their very good friend.

The very next day, Captain Moroni and all his armies attacked the leaderless Lamanite army with great fury, slaughtering them, and they did drive them completely out of the lands of the Nephites restoring peace once again in the thirty and first year of the reign of judges.

After Captain Moroni had fully seen to the strengthening and the fortifications of the lands of the Nephites, he returned to the great city of Zarahemla. He then turned over the command of all the armies to his son, Moronihah, and retired to his own home to live out a well-deserved rest for the remainder of his days.

Commander Helaman also looking forward to a peaceful life, returned to his missionary efforts, and with the aid of his good companions did "establish again the church of God, throughout all the land." In their righteousness, the people again began to prosper and were no longer slow to remember the lord their God, and there was peace in the land.

In the thirty and fifth year of the reign of judges, or about 57 B.C., Commander Helaman the 2nd, the son of Alma the 2nd, died and went "the way of all the earth", leaving his own son to carry on the inherited righteous patrimony of his father's courage and good deeds. (Alma 62:)

One year later, Captain Moroni also died. He left behind him a great and unmatched legacy of leadership, a heroic brilliant military career, and the spiritual fortitude and courage that would never be forgotten even for many, many, centuries to come.

Meanwhile, Commander Helaman the 2nd's brother, Shiblon, a just man, took possession of the sacred records and he walked uprightly before God, as he was faithful in keeping the commandments and serving the Lord. His brother, Corianton, did likewise.

*   *   *

As a note of explanation, Helaman the 1st was one of the sons of the great King Benjamin, but was not particularly significant in Book of Mormon history. Helaman the 2nd, the son of Alma the 2nd, was a prophet, sacred record keeper, a military commander, and the leader of the 2000 stripling warriors, while Helaman the 3rd was his son who became a chief judge and a righteous leader among the Nephite people, and just one more great man in a long line of sacred record keepers.

*   *   *

In the thirty and seventh year of the reign of judges, or about 55 B.C., a large group of Nephites, 5400 men with their wives and children, decided to leave Zarahemla and venture into the land northward. One of them, called Hagoth, had an extreme sense of adventure and was "exceedingly curios" and built an "exceedingly large ship." He built his ship on the borders of Bountiful, near the land of Desolation, and launched it into the west sea by the narrow neck of land. Many of the Nephites went with him in hopes of a new and better life. A year later, the ship returned, and Hagoth built more ships, and took even more people to a place that we know not. Their fate is not known, for they were never heard of again, at least not by the record keepers of the Book of Mormon who supposed, "that they were drowned in the depths of the sea." (Alma 63:7-8)

*   *   *

"The belief that Polynesian ancestry includes Book of Mormon people can be traced back at least to 1851, when George Q. Cannon taught it as a missionary in Hawaii (he was later a counselor in the First Presidency). President Brigham Young detailed the belief in a letter to King Kamehameha V in 1865. Other Church leaders have since affirmed the belief, some indicating that among Polynesian ancestors were the people of Hagoth, who set sail from Nephite lands in approximately 54 B.C. (cf. Alma 63:5-8). In a statement to the Maoris of New Zealand, for instance, President Joseph F. Smith said, "I would like to say to you brethren and sisters . . . you are some of Hagoth's people, and there is NO PERHAPS about it!" (Cole and Jensen, p. 388.) In the prayer offered at the dedication of the Hawaii Temple, President Heber J. Grant referred to the "descendants of Lehi" in Hawaii (IE 23 [Feb. 1920]:283)." Encyclopedia of Mormonism, Vol.3, POLYNESIANS

*   *   *

In the thirty and sixth year of the reign of judges, Shiblon took possession of the sacred records and other sacred items left by his brother, Commander Helaman the 2nd, who had been given the sacred task of safeguarding and writing upon the records by their father Alma the 2nd. Three years later, just before his death, Shiblon conferred the sacred records upon his nephew and then passed on to his own heavenly reward.

Shiblon's younger brother, Corianton, had taken provisions by ship to the people who had gone into the land northward, and had not returned or sent any word. That left only their nephew, Helaman the 3rd, the son of Commander Helaman the 2nd, to carry on the family legacy and to be the soul sacred record keeper. The writings on the sacred records were written down under Helaman's direction and sent out among the people, except the parts which Alma had said should not be sent forth. (Alma 63:12) These things he did while he unknowingly prepared to become an important future leader among the Nephite people.

The 39th year of the judges ended with some of the Nephite dissidents stirring up the chronically threatening and vengeful Lamanites once again to war who came down with numerous warriors to fight with the Nephite army. Captain Moroni's son, the young Captain Moronihah, carried on in his father's foot steps, and as commander of the Nephite armies was able to chase the Lamanite warriors back into their own lands, and once again the Lamanites suffered great losses and were defeated at the hands of the Nephites. This brought to an end the account of Alma and his two sons, Helaman the 2nd and his brother Shiblon. (Alma 63:)

*   *   *

CHAPTER THIRTEEN

* * *

SECRET COMBINATIONS AND OATHS

In the fortieth year of the reign of judges, or about 52 B.C., Chief Judge Pahoran went "the way of all the earth" passing away and leaving behind a power vacuum to be filled in the judgment seat. Three of his sons, Pacumeni, Paanchi, and Pahoran the 2nd, contended over the highly sought after position, this bringing about a great political division among the Nephite people. Finally, by the voice of the people, the young Pahoran was at last chosen to fill the seat. His brother, Paanchi, was very unhappy about this turn of events and he consequently stirred up his own supporters to rebel against the people's decision. This caused great dissension among the people, and he, himself, was apprehended and then put on trial and was sentenced to be executed. His supporters, being extremely angry, now plotted against his brother, the Chief Judge, and sent an assassin called Kishkumen to the young Pahoran's judgment seat. The chosen assassin, in disguise and with swiftness and stealth, executed the young unsuspecting Pahoran as he sat on his judgment seat.

The men, who sent Kishkumen on this mission of death, swore among themselves a secret oath to never reveal the assassin's name or whereabouts. This then was the beginning of a long and wicked tradition of secret combinations. Meanwhile, somewhat by default, but mainly by the voice of the people, the surviving third brother, Pacumeni, was proclaimed to be the new chief judge. (Helaman 1:1-13)

The next year, a very large army of well-armed Lamanites came against the Nephites. The Lamanite King, for his own devious reasons, had appointed a dissenter from among the Nephites, to be their commander. He was a descendent of Zarahemla, "a large and a mighty man" called Coriantumr. He is the third Coriantumr mentioned in the Book of Mormon, Coriantumr the first being son of the Jaredite King Omer, and Coriantumr the 2nd being the last king of the Jaredites.

Being very brash, very confident, and very contemptuous of the Nephites, this Coriantumr led his huge army swiftly and boldly right into the heart of Zarahemla completely surprising the unprepared Nephites who never dreamed that any enemy army would dare attack the great city of Zarahemla itself. Thus the Nephites were thoroughly unprepared for this kind of a surprise attack having deployed the bulk of their armies around the borders of the land. Coriantumr not only attacked and took possession of the great Nephite city of Zarahemla, but being glorified in his own wickedness, he personally killed the young chief judge, Pacumeni.

Continuing in his great impudence and self-confidence, he headed for the city of Bountiful to take the northern parts of the land from the Nephites. What he didn't know was that Chief Captain Moronihah, the son of Captain Moroni, was his equal if not a better commander. Moronihah sent his chief officer, Lehi the 3rd, with his well-trained men to cut off the advancement of Coriantumr. Commander Lehi accomplishing no less, and did chase Coriantumr back towards Zarahemla where Captain Moronihah was waiting to trap Coriantumr's massive Lamanite army between the two Nephite armies. A great bloody battle took place, which resulted in the death of Coriantumr the 3rd, and a significant defeat for his army. The Lamanites retreated to their own lands, and the Nephites under the command of Moronihah retook the city of Zarahemla. The great Nephite city was safe once again, for the time being. (Helaman chapter 1:14-33)

So now in the forty and second year of the reign of the judges, once again the judgment seat was unoccupied. After a certain amount of contention and debate, Helaman the 3rd was chosen by the voice of the people to be the new chief judge.

Although the Book of Mormon heading at the top of Helaman chapter 2 refers to him as Helaman the second because he was the son of commander Helaman, we will refer to him by his book of Mormon index designation, which is Helaman the 3rd, as he is the third Helaman mentioned in the Book of Mormon.

His credentials were solid. He was not only the son of the prophet and the great military leader Commander Helaman, but he was also the grandson of the outstanding missionary, prophet, and sacred record keeper, Alma the younger. All three of these great men, grandfather, father, and son were literal descendents of the legendary Nephi the First, and now it was time for Helaman the 3rd to stand up and show the strength of his heritage and walk in the footsteps of his renowned ancestors.

As one might expect, the secret combinations once again arose being determined to control the judgment seat, and therefore they turned their thoughts to plotting the assassination of the chief judge. The evil assassin, Kishkumen, was brought out of hiding for a repeat performance, just waiting for the right time and place to murder Helaman the 3rd, the new chief judge of the Nephites.

Perhaps, one could possibly argue that even more evil than Kishkumen, was his new boss, a man called Gadianton. The conniving Gadianton had flattered many, promising them high position when he and his secret combination of robbers and murderers took over the government, at which time he would place himself in the judgment seat, a position that he greatly desired. So then true to his evil desires, he sent the vile Kishkumen to assassinate the new chief judge, Helaman the 3rd.

Fortunately, one of Helaman's servants had somehow secretly obtained the information concerning this vile plot, and then acting as a double agent; the servant pretended to cooperate with Kishkumen and led him to the place of the judgment seat. Only minutes before the evil act was to be carried out, the loyal servant stabbed the wicked Kishkumen in the heart ending his fiendish plot and putting a permanent end to his satanic assassin's career.

The servant then reported back to chief judge Helaman the 3rd, and revealed all that had happened. Helaman immediately sent his men to apprehend Gadianton and his robbers and execute them according to law, but they were tipped off and fled secretly into the wilderness, just waiting for their next chance to bring down the Nephite government. (Helaman 2:)

*   *   *

Encyclopedia of Mormonism, Vol.3, OATHS

"Oaths were also used with evil intent. For sinister purposes, the Gadianton robbers and the Jaredites swore secret oaths that had once been sworn by Cain."

*   *   *

For a period of about four years after Kishkumen was killed, the Nephites lived with little contention until the forty and sixth year of the reign of judges. At that time, there arose widespread dissension, much hatred, and a great contention among the Nephite people. This led to a situation of great anxiety and fearfulness among many Nephites who decided there must be a better place to live. So they packed up their things and traveled "an exceedingly great distance, insomuch that they came to large bodies of water and many rivers" into the lands northward. These lands in the north had always been referred to as the "the lands of desolation" because of the great destruction that had come upon the ancient Jaredite people who had previously lived there. However over many hundreds of years, the land itself had mostly recovered and was no longer desolate, although the forests were still less than lush. The new inhabitants were very conscious of the need to take care of the land and now cared for the new growth and protected "..whatsoever tree should spring up upon the face of the land that it should grow up.." (Helaman 3:9) And the people did multiply and spread over the face of the land and they covered the land northward from "sea south to the sea north, from the sea west to the sea east." (Helaman 3:8)

*   *   *

If you interpret the above scripture literally, it sounds as though the Nephites lived on a large island. Certainly this description in the above scripture would preclude any real estate in the Palmyra New York area, but in the description there is a clue as to the contorted shape of the isthmus on which the Nephites had built a civilization, very possibly at the narrow isthmus of southern Mexico. In the land of Lehi-Nephi, the sea west was to the west, but when they moved up to Zarahemla, the west sea was now the sea south relative to their new location. Their way of expressing descriptive geography in their culture would surely have been somewhat different from ours. Never the less, the isthmus of Tehuantepec in southern Mexico not only can be made to fit many scriptures regarding Book of Mormon geography, but it also fits climate and seasonal clues, as well as geological phenomenon such as earthquakes and volcanoes, and it seems to fit the clues regarding overland distances and travel times on foot.

* * *

There in the lands of desolation, which were denuded of timber by the previous civilization, some Nephites lived in tents but many begin to skillfully build houses and all manner of buildings of cement becoming exceedingly expert in this particular manner of building. They also built well-crafted ships, as well as temples, sanctuaries, and synagogues, that were supplemented by lumber shipped from the southlands. (Helaman 3:3-12)

Many Book of Mormon critics have laughed at the idea of Indians in Central America using cement to build their houses and other structures. President Heber J. Grant tells an interesting antidote relating to that criticism.

* * *

President Heber J. Grant, Gospel Standards, p.28

Said President Grant: "When I was a young unmarried man, another young man who had received a doctor's degree ridiculed me for believing in the Book of Mormon. He said he could point out two lies in that book. One was that the people had built their homes out of cement, and they were very skillful in the use of cement. He said there had never been found and never would be found, a house built of cement by the ancient inhabitants of this country, because the people in that early age knew nothing about cement."

"Not very far from the City of Mexico there is a monument two hundred and ten feet high, built of cement . . . . My first counselor [Anthony W. Ivins] has stood on that monument. You could put forty tabernacles like this one inside of it. It covers more than ten acres of ground and is two and a half times higher than this building. From the top of that monument one can see small mounds, and as these mounds are being uncovered, they are found to be wonderfully built cement houses, with drain pipes of cement, showing skill and ability, superior almost to anything we have today so far as the use of cement is concerned."

(Selections from the Sermons and Writings of President Heber J. Grant Compiled by G. Homer Durham 1943 by The Improvement Era)

*   *   *

Many of the righteous and converted Lamanites who were now called the people of Ammon, also went forth to the land northward and became a part of that community along with the people residing in that land. A few of the Nephite people attempted to be righteous, but the majority of the Nephites during this time period in the Book of Mormon committed all sorts of abominations, whoredoms, and even the plundering and the murder of their fellow citizens.

A profusion of books and records "which are particular and very large" recorded all the activities and the proceedings of both the Lamanite and the Nephite people during these contentious times. They had been "handed down from one generation to another by the Nephites" as specific writers wrote and protected these writings. It should be noted that most of this proliferation of records was recorded and preserved chiefly by the Nephites. Due to a number of extenuating circumstances though, not even a hundredth part of these writings made it into the pages of the Book of Mormon, or at least that is certainly the implication as it is recorded in Helaman 3:14.

*   *   *

CHAPTER FOURTEEN

* * *

NEPHI AND LEHI

Back in Zarahemla, chief judge Helaman the 3rd, the son of commander Helaman, walked in the ways of his father and judged the people with "justice and equity." Understandably, he doted on his two sons who were named after ancestral Nephite heroes, the eldest being Nephi the 2nd and the younger one Lehi the 4th. Both of them grew in spiritual might and did become good and righteous men walking in the steps of their righteous and illustrious ancestors and they did do honor to their heritage.

During this time, the Nephite people enjoyed great prosperity because of their righteousness and their obedience to the Lord's commandments. Chief Judge Helaman and those in the proper authority baptized tens of thousands in to the church.

Only the seductive temptation of pride in their riches and the insidious lure of their desire to be of high position in their church stature would cause them to eventually come to corruption in their good standing with the Lord, and bring much contention to the community. Slowly, but surely, contention arose as some of the richer people began to persecute and show flagrant disrespect to the poor among them. The rich being steeped in their pride, perceived the poor to be a lesser sort of human bean and certainly not worthy of the valuable time or respect of the upper class.

In the fifty and third year of the reign of judges, or about 41 B.C., Chief Judge Helaman the 3rd passed away, leaving his eldest son, Nephi the 2nd, to reign in his stead, whereas his son did take that legal position in the judgment seat. So it came to pass then, that this new chief judge, Nephi the 2nd, followed in his father's footsteps and did strive to judge fairly, and he did keep the Lord's commandments and was a just man. (Helaman 3:)

Unfortunately, the Nephite people, mainly due their great prosperity and pride, quickly deteriorated into a transgressing, sinful, and boastful people. Despite the sincere and almost desperate preaching of Nephi and his brother Lehi, the people continued in their disobedience to the Lord's commandments and in their selfish wicked pursuits. They even ignored the admonishments of their Nephite military commander, Moronihah. So, once again we see history repeat itself, as they brought upon themselves through their own disobedience and prideful acts, a justified punishment and they were "afflicted and smitten, and driven before the Lamanites." (Helaman 4:13)

Nephi "had become weary because of their iniquity" as he watched his people become stiff-necked, and ungovernable. He was thoroughly discouraged and greatly disappointed as he observed that the wicked did outnumber the righteous. Feeling disheartened and somewhat hopeless, he never the less felt obligated, even compelled to do something about it.

Nine years after Nephi the 2nd had taken the judgment seat, he became so "weary" at the state of his people, that he gave up the judgment seat and handed it over to a man called Cezoram. In the era of the Chief Judge Cezoram's leadership, the people fell into great transgression, corrupted the laws, became "grossly wicked" and rejected righteous teaching of any kind.

Before he had passed away, Nephi the 2nd's father, Helaman the 3rd, had spoken to his sons and reminded them of their great heritage and the greatness of their heroic forefathers for whom they were named. At that time, he admonished his sons to follow in the footsteps of their righteous ancestors and to proceed with the business of "going about doing good." Nephi felt an obligation to his heritage and to his own father and so therefore was inspired to carry out his father's last wishes, which was for his sons to use their energy to change things among the people and to bring them to their God. Accordingly then, Nephi following his heart and with the support of his brother Lehi, who felt the same way, began to "go about doing good" and proceeded to preach the word of the Lord to the people for the rest of their days. (Helaman 5:4)

Despite Nephi and Lehi's good intentions and the sincerity of their words, the Nephite people steadily declined in their morality as they became prideful, committed adultery, oppressed the poor, stole and lied, and continued "making a mock of that which was sacred." Some of the dissenters among them fled to the Lamanites, stirred up hatred towards their own Nephite people, and became traitors as they joined the Lamanite armies in their invasion of the lands of the Nephite people.

Needless to say, the Lord was not pleased with the Nephites, nor did he protect them in their wickedness, and so in the fifty and eighth year of the judges, the Lamanites were able to take over the lands of Zarahemla all the way to the borders of Bountiful. There, Captain Moronihah and his army were able to hold on to that part of the Nephite lands. Never the less, the people were not worthy of the Lord's protection "And thus had they fallen into this great transgression; yea, thus had they become weak, because of their transgression in the space of not many years." (Helaman 4:26)

Nephi the 2nd and his brother Lehi the 4th went from city to city in the lands of Zarahemla, where many Lamanites now lived, and due to the great power and authority by which the two brothers preached, they were able to miraculously convert an amazing number of converts, which was over eight thousand worthy Lamanites. Their work was not done, however. Proceeding on in their great quest for saving souls, they eventually found themselves in the land of Nephi, which was to the south of the "narrow strip of wilderness", where they looked for a new field to harvest.

Here in this land, the Lamanites did not receive them in the same way that they had been received in the north, basically just being ignored. In this land of Nephi, they were taken and thrown in the very same prison in which Ammon the 1st and his men had been imprisoned many years earlier by the guards of King Limhi. The Lamanites here were truly cruel and murderous. So after starving Nephi and Lehi many days, the Lamanites decided to kill them, but the executioners were absolutely astonished as they went to lay hold upon the two gallant missionaries. The guards found that they were unable to lay their hands upon their prisoners, as the two were now completely encircled by fire. Then the two missionaries spoke saying, "Fear not, for behold it is God that has shown unto you this marvelous thing in which is shown unto you that ye cannot lay your hands on us to slay us." (Helaman 5:26)

The prison walls shook and trembled and a cloud of darkness came over and threw its shadow over these spiritually lost Lamanites, as well as the rebellious Nephite dissenters among them. Then a voice above the dark cloud spoke to them saying, "Repent ye, repent ye, and seek no more to destroy my servants who I have sent unto you to declare good tidings." (Helaman 5:29)

The walls shook and trembled again, and again, and the voice repeated the message three times. Then one of the men among the Nephite dissenters, a man called Aminadab, brought the crowd's attention to the shining faces of the two missionaries who were looking skyward and seemed to be talking to heavenly beings. The Lamanites and Nephite dissenters were overcome with great fear, until the newly reformed Aminiadab convinced them that they must all repent and have faith in Christ. Then in humbleness and fear, the crowd cried unto the heavenly voice for their deliverance. The cloud was removed from them, and they all, every soul was then encircled by fire with Nephi and Lehi in the midst of them, and they were all "ministered" to by angels. About three hundred souls were converted to Christ and went about the land declaring what they had seen, and as a result, they converted even more Lamanites to lay down their arms, and give back all the lands of the Nephites that they had taken. (Helaman 5:)

By 29 B.C., the majority of the Lamanites were converted to Christ and they had become more righteous than the "grossly wicked" Nephites. Many of the Lamanites went among the Nephite people in Zarahemla and testified to them with great spiritual strength and tried to exhort them to repentance.

During this period of time, the Nephites and the Lamanites intermingled and had free dealings with each other, benefiting both peoples until they were all prospering in the land, perhaps a little too well, for this would eventually contribute to the degeneration of their beliefs and the destruction of their society.

In the sixty and sixth year of the reign of the judges, chief judge Cezarom was murdered, and his son who succeeded him was also assassinated in the judgment seat, both of them by the Gadianton robbers. In order to gain power and riches, many of the Nephites and the wicked among the Lamanites, had entered into secret oaths and covenants with the Gadianton robbers; and so consequently, the robbers and murderers were shielded from punishment by their own law officials and literally did get away with murder.

The righteous among the Lamanites attempted to rid the communities of the robbers, but it was futile while the robbers were protected by widespread conspiracy among the more part of the Nephites who partook of the spoils and entered into oaths and secret combinations. The spirit of the Lord withdrew from the corrupt Nephites, while the Lamanites walked "in truth and uprightness before him." By 23 B.C., the government was completely corrupt, having been completely taken over by the wicked among the Nephites and the menacing Gadianton robbers. Meanwhile, the rule of law in the land as well as all decency and the rights of the righteous poor, were unsympathetically trampled beneath the feet of the wicked. (Helaman 6:)

*   *   *

Encyclopedia of Mormonism, Vol.3, SECRET COMBINATIONS

"In the Book of Mormon, several secret combinations challenged governments ruled by the "voice of the people" or by righteous kings. . . . they were a threat to the Nephite and Lamanite nations when the Gadianton combinations, over a period of many years, challenged the constituted authorities and eventually seized power. The concerted effort of the whole populace later defeated the Gadiantons, but others rose in their place. The Book of Mormon details the tactics and strategies of the Gadiantons, mentions a variety of countermeasures, and shows that a secret combination was responsible for the final downfall of the Nephites."

* * *

In our modern society, we make no distinction between the two words robbers and thieves, as they both have basically the same meaning to us. The Bible too makes no distinction between the two words, nor did any of the contemporaries of Joseph Smith's time. This common lack of distinction between robbers and thieves is not true in the Book of Mormon, nor in Near Eastern Law. In these particular cultures, robbers and thieves are two distinctly different designations for two different types of criminals.

In the Semitic culture of the Book of Mormon people, a thief was one who stole from his neighbor and was then punished for what was considered a comparatively minor offense by the local law. A robber, on the other hand, was a dangerous outsider, part of a gang of robbers, whose violence and destruction did much more harm than just stealing, and consequently, they were dealt with by the military and often hastily executed.

Bernard S. Jackson, a Professor of Law at the University of Kent-Canterbury and editor of the Jewish Law Annual explains how in the Book of Mormon, robbers usually acted as organized groups going against local governments and even attacking entire towns. "They swore oaths and extorted ransom, and they were a menace far worse than ordinary criminals. Thieves, however, were a much less serious threat to society and not dealt with as harshly as the menacing robbers." [Bernard S. Jackson, Theft in Early Jewish Law (Oxford: Oxford University Press, 1972)].

This subtle difference between the words thieves and robbers, as specifically illustrated in this ancient culture, would have been highly unlikely to have been known by Joseph Smith, nor even thought of by him, and certainly not inferred in his own writing if he had actually fabricated the Book of Mormon based on his own knowledge and that of his contemporaries.

*   *   *

Encyclopedia of Mormonism, Vol.1, BOOK OF MORMON, HISTORY OF WARFARE "The Gadianton robbers typically raided towns, avoided open conflict, made terrorizing demands, and secretly assassinated government officials." These robbers were more than just thieves. They were an evil corrupting menace, a cancer on that society.

*   *   *

After a very disappointing trip to the land northward to preach and prophesy to the people there, and then being rejected by them, Nephi the 2nd, the son of chief judge Helaman the 3rd, returned to the land of Zarahemla. Zarahemla was in a terrible state of affairs with the Gadianton robbers having usurped all authority and had even taken over the judgment seat. Lawbreakers were going completely unpunished, and the Nephite people were lying, stealing, committing adultery, and even murder. It was utter chaos among the Nephites in Zarahemla at this time.

Because of all this, Nephi's heart was "swollen with sorrow within his breast." In his grief, he went up to a tower by the highway, which led to the chief market place in Zarahemla and began to pour out his soul to God and to mourn for the people. This caused a crowd to gather and to marvel as to why he mourned so greatly. He took the opportunity to point out their iniquities and most grievous sins and how they had set their hearts upon riches and the praise of men. He told them to repent or "..he shall scatter you forth that ye shall become meat for dogs and wild beast." (Helaman 7: 19) He told them if they did not repent, the Lord would not protect them from their enemies, and Zarahemla and all the lands of their possession would be taken from them, and they would "..be destroyed from off the face of the earth." (Helaman 7:28)

* * *

"Chief Markets. No one knowledgeable of pre-Columbian Mexico has had any doubt that markets were found in all sizeable settlements.

Cortez and his fellows were amazed by the market in Tlatelolco in the Valley of Mexico, by its diversity of goods, and by the complexity of its organization. Yet until recently, only little attention has been given to the fact that a number of these cities had multiple markets. Tenochititlan, has established that each major sector of the city had its own market, in addition to the giant central one. Apparently Zarahemla was no different."

(See http://www.jefflindsay.com/BMEvidences.shtml)

* * *

Once again, the Book of Mormon offhandedly relates information and knowledge that would have been highly unlikely to have been known by Joseph Smith, a farm boy with a rudimentary education, nor would it have been very likely for such obscure knowledge to have been known even by the contemporary college professors of those times.

*   *   *

The corrupt judges who belonged to the secret band of Gadianton were very angry with Nephi the 2nd because he had been telling the people how corrupt their laws and leaders were, and they were very upset that he had accused them of "secret works of darkness." The wicked judges, however, did not dare lay their hands upon him, as they were afraid as to how the people might react to his persecution by a corrupt government, so they tried to turn the people against him publicly and to stir up anger against him. Some of the people believed in the words of Nephi the 2nd, and cried out that he should be left alone and that he could not have known the things he spoke of, unless he was a prophet.

Soon after, Nephi was inspired to speak to them, and he reminded them of how Abraham, Moses, Zenos, and Zenock and many other prophets had testified of the coming of Christ, and asked them how they could after all this, still reject the testimonies and witnesses and evidences of the truth of Christ and the Day of Judgment.

He then shocked them by announcing that the Day of Judgment was at hand, as even at this very moment, the chief judge was being murdered by his own brother. Both brothers belonged to the secret band of Gadianton robbers. (Helaman 8;)

More than just a little curious, there were five men who raced to the judgment seat to check the truth of what Nephi had said. They were astonished to find that the chief judge really was dead lying in his own blood, and fear came upon them and they fell to the earth as they perceived that all that Nephi had said would truly come to pass. When the people came and saw that the chief judge was dead and that there were five men lying at his feet, they supposed that God had struck these five murderers to the earth for punishment and so they took them and cast them into prison.

Meanwhile, the corrupt judges decided to question the five prisoners. The five witnesses then testified that Nephi the 2nd had foretold the murder of the chief judge. The judges then suspected collusion, thinking Nephi had agreed with some co-conspirator to kill the chief judge, and then pretended that he had prophesied the heinous deed by spiritual power, all in order to trick the people into believing he was a prophet. In light of the new suspicions, the five suspects were released, while Nephi was bound and taken before the people to be interrogated by the corrupt judges as they thought that they might cross him in his own words.

Nephi rebuked them and their accusations, and told them that he would show them another sign that they might know of the truth. He told them to go to the house of Seantum, the brother of chief judge Seezoram, and ask him about any agreements that he had made with Nephi, and whether he had killed the judge, which Seantum would then deny, of course. Then Nephi told them that they should examine the skirts of Seantum's cloak where they would find the blood stains of the victim on the hem, the victim being his very own brother, Seezoram.

Seantum was then sought out and interrogated, and just as predicted, he did deny the heinous crime, until they discovered the blood upon the hem of his cloak, at which point, with great guilt and fear he confessed everything and cleared Nephi of any wrong doing. Due to Seantum's confession and the testimonies of the accused five, some of the people were sure that Nephi the 2nd was a true prophet, while others even supposed that he was a God, lest he could not have known all that he had revealed. (Helaman 9:)

After this incident, the people were divided in their support of Nephi, and he was left alone to ponder in his own house the things that the Lord had shown him. While he was pondering and lamenting the state of the people, a voice came to him saying that because of his "unwearyingness" in declaring the word of the Lord, that he would not only be greatly blessed, but that he would receive the power to smite the earth with famine and pestilence and the "..power that whatsoever ye shall seal on earth shall be sealed in heaven . . ." Then the Lord commanded him to go to the people and declare that they must repent or be destroyed. He went from multitude to multitude warning them and declaring the word of God, but in their hardened hearts, they reviled him and would not hearken to his words. In their fallen state, they became so wicked that they were divided against themselves and there was much contention to the point that they began to slay each other with the sword. (Helaman 10:)

A year later, things had deteriorated to the point that Nephi was sure that the people would completely annihilate themselves by the sword, so he asked the Lord to send a famine that it might humble them and turn them to their God.

And thus there was a great famine, which came upon the land, lasting for nearly three years, and killing thousands before the people finally submitted and humbled themselves before the Lord. They begged Nephi as a man of God, to turn away the famine. In light of their humbleness and repentance, and the fact that they had stamped out the Gadianton robbers, Nephi pleaded with the Lord to turn aside the famine and "send forth rain upon the face of the earth" that the earth might bring forth her fruits and grains. The Lord granted Nephi's request in the seventy and sixth year, or about 16

B.C., and the rain came upon the earth once again to provide bounty for the people as they rejoiced and glorified God. In their gratitude, they recognized and esteemed Nephi the 2nd and his brother Lehi the 4th as prophets and men of God, who received revelations daily. (Helaman 11:23)

Peace and prosperity prevailed for the next four years. Unfortunately, some groups of people just cannot tolerate or be satisfied with having peace and prosperity. A certain number of Nephite dissenters had joined with and stirred up certain Lamanites to revive the secrets of the Gadianton robbers, and once again, they began to rob, plunder, and murder. The numbers among the robbers greatly increased and they infested the mountains and the wilderness, until they were able to actually defy the large armies that were sent to eradicate them. Meantime, they continued in their crimes, committing murders, kidnapping women and children, and bringing great fear upon the land. Unfortunately, the people had once again forgotten God and "they began to wax strong in iniquity" and therefore by 7 B.C., they were once more very ripe for the destruction that would soon come upon a stubborn and an unrepentant people. (Helaman 11:)

*   *   *

Helaman Chapter 12 is an unusual and an unaccredited insert by Mormon nearly four hundred years later, as he abridges the large plates in the book of Helaman. He says, "..yea, we can see that the lord in his great infinite goodness doth bless and prosper those who put their trust in him." As Mormon then editorializes his observations on God's power and men's weaknesses, he comments on how in his own observations, it seems that when the Lord is blessing the people the most, that is the time when they harden their hearts and remember him the least. Lamenting their ignorance, he writes "How foolish, and how evil, and devilish . . . and how slow to do good, are the children of men . . ." and how quick they are ". . . to set their hearts upon the vain things of the world! . . . Behold they do not desire that the Lord their God, who hath created them, should rule and reign over them . . ." (Helaman Chapter 12)

Mormon ponders in amazement at the arrogance of human beings and how in the "nothingness of the children of men" they ignore and disobey the Lord's commandments while they seem completely oblivious to the fact that ". . . at his voice do the hills and mountains tremble and quake" and by ". . . his voice doth the whole earth shake." He says that the children of men are "..less than the dust of the earth", because at least the dust of the earth will obey and move "hither and thither" according to the command of "our great and everlasting God."

Sounding somewhat cynical about human behavior in general, and certainly incredulous concerning the actions of many of the Lord's chosen who had been taught better, he then makes a poignant statement, if not a very sad truth:

*　　*　　*

"And thus we see that except the Lord doth chasten his people with many afflictions, yea, except he doth visit them with death and with terror, and with famine and with all manner of pestilence, they will not remember him." (Helaman 12:3)

* * *

The capriciousness of human decision making, the weakness of their resolve to follow the commandments, and their self-indulgence and rash choices when faced with temptation, must greatly disappoint the Lord at times. No wonder, he has to remind his children of the importance of keeping the commandments with occasional unhappy and tragic occurrences in their lives. He therefore has to do something to get their attention back on the right track and to get their spiritual priorities back in line with the great plan of redemption.

Mormon points out that because of these human frailties, the Lord has declared that; "for this cause that men might be saved, hath repentance been declared." He praises those who will change their lives for the Lord, and says that blessed are those who repent and hearken to the voice of their God. Then he declares that if it were up to him, he would have it that all men should be saved. However, he reminds us that unfortunately the scriptures say that in the great and last day, there inevitably will be those who will not recognize or respect God's power and so will then be cast out from the presence of the Lord. He concludes by saying, "They that have done good shall have everlasting life; and they that have done evil shall have everlasting damnation. And thus it is. Amen." (Helaman 12:26)

* * *

CHAPTER FIFTEEN

* * *

SAMUEL THE LAMANITE

In the eighty and sixth year of the reign of the judges, or about 6 B.C., during a time of great wickedness among the Nephites, a Lamanite prophet came out of the midst of those truly converted, obedient, and righteous Lamanite people that he lived among, to take his journey into the land of Zarahemla. He was called Samuel the Lamanite, and he did endeavor to call to repentance and warn the Nephite people. With zeal and real sincerity, he expressed a great deal of concern for their impending destruction. Unfortunately he had little success, as they forthrightly rejected all his words. Disappointed, he started to head towards his own land when the voice of the Lord came to him and commanded him to return to the Nephite people in the great city of Zarahemla and to prophesy to them and warn them again. This he obediently did. Alas, they wouldn't even let him into the city, let alone preach to them. So he stood upon the wall of the city and cried out with a loud voice "..and prophesied unto the people whatsoever things the Lord put into his heart."

*   *   *

Spencer W. Kimball, Conference Report, April 1954, p.105

"Would those who scorn the Indian and deprive him of the blessings remember how the Lord loves his Lamanites and how he told his first leaders in this dispensation to journey among the Lamanites. And it shall be given thee . . . what thou shalt do. (D. & C. 28:14-15.) In the days immediately preceding the coming of the Lord, even the Lamanite Prophet Samuel felt the sting and smart of the caustic discriminations when he said: "And now, because I am a Lamanite, and have spoken unto you the words which the Lord commanded me, and because it was hard against you, ye are angry with me and do seek to destroy me, and have cast me out from among you." (Helaman 14:10.)

*   *   *

Despite the people's unwarranted persecution and barbaric treatment of Samuel the Lamanite, he proceeded with the work that he was commanded to do among them. He warned them of a man who would come among them with flattering words and say that they should do whatsoever their hearts should desire for there is no iniquity, and they therefore would not suffer for it. He said that the people would lift up this man and give him their substance and riches, but their riches would be cursed, and one day they would cry out to the Lord, but unfortunately, the day of their probation will have passed. (Helaman 13):

Samuel told the people that in five years hence, the Son of God would come to earth and then redeem all those that did believe on his name. As a sign to the people, he told them that there would be great lights in the heavens and no darkness when the night came, and there would be two days and a night without any darkness. He also said there would be the sign of a new star rising, a star which no one had ever seen before. This then would mark the coming of the Son of God.

Then he told them, that Christ himself must die in order to bring about the redemption, the resurrection, and the salvation of mankind. There would also be great signs that would mark the death of the Son of God. These signs would come from the heavens where the sun, and the moon, and the stars would refuse to give their light to man for the space of three days. There would also be "thunderings and lightnings" as the earth, itself, would tremble and brake up, and this great upheaval in the earth would manifest itself in the great devastation of mountains, valleys, and the widespread destruction of cities and highways.

Lastly, he told them that there would be a righteous judgment come upon all those who believed in Christ, and an equally just judgment would come upon those whosoever did not believe in Christ, for God had given men the knowledge to know good from evil, and he made men free to choose for themselves, whether it be iniquity or righteousness. (Helaman 14:)

Samuel then continues to remind the Nephite people that unless they repent, it shall be better for the Lamanites "than for you except ye repent." The Lamanites had not been taught righteousness and at least had somewhat of an excuse in being led down the wrong path because of the wrong teachings and traditions of their fathers. Consequently the Lord promised that although the Lamanites would be smitten, abused, and scattered, that in the end, he would not utterly destroy them.

On the other hand, the Nephite people who had been taught well, who had known the Lord, who had been brought to righteousness and prosperity many times by their great prophets, who had been greatly blessed by the Lord, but then still had rejected the Lord because they were more interested in riches and the praise of men; all these would find themselves under a whole different set of consequences. He warned the Nephites, again, repeating the Lord's words; "If they will not repent, and observe to do my will, I will utterly destroy them . . ." (Helaman 15:17)

Although many Nephites believed the words of Samuel the Lamanite and sought out Nephi the 2nd to confess their sins and be baptized, the majority of them violently rejected Samuel and so did cast stones and arrows at him as he stood upon the wall.

Even so, there were many who did realize that Samuel was actually being protected from the stones and arrows as he stood there on the wall unharmed, so they began to believe and to seek after baptism. Unfortunately, though, the more part of the people attributed their inability to hit Samuel as the work of the devil and so they tried to take him by force and bind him. Samuel being fleet of foot, jumped from the wall and fled back to his own country where he became a prophet to his own people, never to be heard of again among the Nephites.

The next five years passed by quickly as the more part of the unrepentant Nephites wallowed in their own pride, immorality, dishonesty, and were in general, steeped in wickedness. In the ninetieth year of the reign of the judges, or about 2 B.C., Samuel the Lamanite's words began to come to pass, as "there were great signs given unto the people, and wonders, and the words of the prophets began to be fulfilled."

Though difficult for one to believe, the hard hearted and wicked among the Nephites passed the signs off as just mere coincidence. They said that they could not see what was happening in Jerusalem with their own eyes to know if this mythical Christ was really born, and it was not reasonable to believe in it. They said it was nothing more than just a "wicked tradition" which had been handed down by their fathers to keep them all in ignorance so that they would be servants to their father's words. "Yea, why will he not show himself in this land as well as in the land of Jerusalem?" (Helaman 16:19) The people, in general, ignored the signs and wonders, and they were skeptical of the miracles due to the great hold that Satan had upon their hearts, and thus this unhappy situation prevailed throughout the land in 1 B.C. as we come to the end of the book of Helaman, all this according to Helaman and his son's own records.

*   *   *

Bruce R. McConkie, Mormon Doctrine, p.730 SIGNS OF THE TIMES REFUSAL OF MEN TO BELIEVE SIGNS OF TIMES.—The very fact that men refuse to believe the many signs of the times is itself one of the signs promised to precede the advent of our Lord. Peter prophesied of this, saying: "There shall come in the last days scoffers, walking after their own lusts, And saying, Where is the promise of his coming? for since the fathers fell asleep, all things continue as they were from the beginning of the creation." (2 Pet. 3:3-4.) That is, in effect, these scoffers are saying, "Why be so gullible as to believe that earthquakes, floods, famines, pestilence, wars, iniquity, and all similar conditions are signs of the last days? Have not these same conditions existed from the beginning of time?"

*   *   *

While it is true that the skeptics can claim that there have always been wars and rumors of wars, as well as calamities, floods, and earthquakes in diverse places, there will be other signs that are not so vague or common. These will accompany some of the wars and calamities, but these particular signs have not appeared many times throughout history, and will be distinctive unto themselves. These signs will be signs that cannot be disregarded, nor considered common or coincidence, nor can they be lightly passed over and ignored, at least by none except the most harden hearts.

One such sign, regarding wars and rumors of wars as a sign of the times, involves a prophesy of Joseph Smith which happened nearly thirty years before the Civil War ever began. Joseph Smith prophesied in detail that there would be a war that would start in South Carolina, that it would be between the North and the South, that Great Britain would be brought into it, that it would involve slavery, and it would result in the death and misery of many souls.

This was not just the vague prediction of a "soothsayer", or just some lucky guess. Its uncanny detail and its historical accuracy in describing what would actually happen three decades before the future Civil War is astounding to say the least, and to those spiritually in tune, this is quite obviously an inspired prophesy. (see D&C 87:)

There are other signs that are hard to explain away as just coincidence. Even when you consider all the great tribulations brought upon the House of Israel by the Assyrians, the Babylonian conquest, and the rule of the Romans, even greater tribulations are spoken of by Christ in the first chapter of JS-Matthew. He said that in the last days there would be tribulations like never before sent upon Israel as a sign before his coming.

In our modern times, Nazi Germany systematically exterminated six million innocent Jewish men, women, and children, simply because they were Jews. More recently, many nations of the Middle East have violently fought against the very existence of the Modern State of Israel. Palestinian extremists continually rain rockets upon innocent civilians in Israel, while the leader of Iran even called for the annihilation of Israel from off the face of the planet. Sadly, we have most definitely not seen an end to these signs of great tribulations that will come upon the House of Israel in the last days.

Even so, the prophets through out the scriptures have prophesied that there would be the sign of the Gathering of Israel in the last days, lo even from the four corners of the earth. In spite of the violent objections of its enemies, in 1948, the modern state of Israel was established in Palestine beginning the political gathering of Israel from the four corners of the earth. This was certainly something new, an unprecedented event, and one of the signs that had never been seen before.

The spiritual gathering of Israel and their recognition of Jesus Christ as the Messiah seems to be in a much slower state of progress with somewhat of a ways to go. Nevertheless, some modern Jews have at least started to recognize that Jesus Christ was a great teacher and possibly even a prophet.

Another sign of the last days, as stated in Joseph Smith Mathew 1:31, is that the gospel of Jesus Christ "shall be preached in all the world, for a witness unto all nations, and then shall the end come." During the term of the presidency of our beloved prophet President Gordon B. Hinckley, we saw the LDS church become a truly international church with more members outside the United States than within. We've seen an army of more than 50,000 missionaries preaching the gospel of Jesus Christ "in all the world, for a witness unto all nations", not to mention that the number of temples that have been built and dedicated around the globe have now been tripled.

President Thomas S. Monson, continuing in that same vein of great worldwide progress, has with dedication and enthusiasm moved ahead with some of the same energy as President Hinckley, seeing to it that the prophesies concerning the growth of the church shall be fulfilled.

The Lord has declared that not even the angels in heaven shall know the hour and the day that he shall come, never-the-less, those who are familiar with the scriptures and in tune with the Lord's spirit, will recognize the signs of his coming and will be ready with oil in their lamps for that day when the Bridegroom doth come.

*   *   *

"Wherefore, be faithful, praying always, having your lamps trimmed and burning, and oil with you, that you may be ready at the coming of the Bridegroom."

"For behold, verily, verily, I say unto you, that I come quickly. Even so, Amen"

D&C 33:17 & 18

*   *   *

CHAPTER SIXTEEN

*   *   *

THE DAYS OF CHRIST UPON
THE EARTH

In the ninety and first year of the reign of judges, which was 600 years from the time that Lehi left Jerusalem, the good and wise Chief Judge Lachoneus was governor over all the land of the Nephites. During this time, Nephi the 2nd, son of Helaman, turned over to his eldest son, Nephi the 3rd, the plates of brass and all other sacred records, and then departed out of the land to where "no man knoweth." (3 Nephi 1:3)

A year later, or in about 1 A.D., despite the prophesies and great signs and miracles that were being beheld, many of the Nephites began to say that the time which Samuel the Lamanite had prophesied about had come and gone and there had been no such thing as a day without a night. Therefore they rejoiced thinking that they were safe from utter destruction, and all these things that he had prophesized had not happened, and they had not even had to repent after all.

All the scoffers and those stubborn nonbelievers began to single out the good people who still believed that the prophecies would actually come to pass. Then these wicked ones persecuted the good people. These vile skeptics indulging themselves in their own wicked delights, then set aside a special day for the execution of all those who still foolishly believed in this mythical Christ and his so called great judgment day.

Nephi the 3rd, now taking over for his father, Nephi the 2nd, was extremely sorrowful about these events and he bowed himself down and cried mightily all that day to the Lord to save the faithful believers from the great evil of this planned execution. After praying all day, the voice of the Lord came unto him and said be of "good cheer" because on this very night, the sign of the coming of the Son of God will appear and He will be born to the world on the morrow.

When night came and it was time for the sun to go down, darkness did not come, and so it was that the night was as if it was day and the people were astonished. Seeing this, many of the nonbelievers began to realize that they had made a big mistake and they fell upon the earth as if they were dead, and all the people from east to west and from north to south, from all over the land, recognized that truly the son of God was about to come into the world. The next day, the sun arose and the people realized that there really had been a new star the night before that arose in the heavens and that no one had ever seen before. So all those signs prophesied by Samuel the Lamanite concerning Christ's birth, that the skeptics had denied and the faithful had looked for, were now fulfilled.

Despite all this, Satan had such a hold on many of the hardhearted scoffers that they tried to convince the rest of the people that all this was just coincidence and the signs meant absolutely nothing. Nevertheless, the more part of the people did believe and were converted and were baptized by Nephi the 3rd. Even the those who had stirred up contention "endeavoring to prove by the scriptures that it was no more expedient to observe the Law of Moses" due to the birth of the Savior, saw the err of their interpretation and had a change of heart and they were also converted. (3 Nephi 1:24)

For the next few years there was relative peace upon the land, except for the Gadianton robbers in the mountains, who continued to steal and commit murder, and they also did entice and recruit some of the Nephite dissenters. They were even able to recruit some of the unsuspecting youth of the righteous Lamanites. (3 Nephi 1:)

In a surprisingly short time, the Nephite people soon began to doubt the wonders and miracles and signs of Christ's birth that they had seen with their own eyes, even attributing these things to the devil deceiving them, where in reality, it was he that was causing them to doubt. By the thirteenth year after Christ's birth, the Nephite people were back into the depths of wickedness. The Gadianton robbers had rose to new heights of carnage and waste upon the people with their vastly increased numbers. The situation became so desperate, that for their own survival, the wicked Nephites joined forces with the righteous Lamanites to drive the robbers back into the mountains. The righteous Lamanites who joined the Nephites were numbered with the Nephites and their young men and their young women became exceedingly fair and white. (3 Nephi 2:)

In the sixteenth year after Christ's birth, the new leader of the Gadiantion robbers, Giddianhi, wrote a letter to Lachoneus the Governor of the land, saying that as commander of the robbers, he commanded thousands who were ready to come down out of the hills upon the Nephites with great vengeance and utterly destroy them, but he hoped that it would not be necessary. In a supposed spirit of compromise, the cunning Giddianhi said that he would swear an oath that if the Nephites would surrender and yield all that they possessed and turn over all their lands to the Gadianton robbers, that the robbers would then accept the Nephites into their own ranks and spare their lives, providing of course, that the Nephites would swear and oath of allegiance to the robbers.

Governor Lachoneus was so incensed by the arrogance and the utter insolence of the robber leader, that he refused to even acknowledge the proposal. Instead, he sent a proclamation throughout the land for all the people to gather their flocks, their herds, and their property, all together in one spot, so that fortifications could be built and thus the Nephite armies would be able to protect the Nephite people and their possessions. Furthermore, Governor Lachoneus also called the people to repentance and prophesied among them, and the people were inspired by his words and obeyed him. Meanwhile, Lachoneus organized his men appointing captains and chief captains to lead his armies.

In the tradition of Captain Moroni and his son Moronihah, a great and skilled commander and prophet, Gidgiddoni, was called to command the Nephite army. This Nephite commander Gidgiddoni should not be confused with the robber leader, Giddianhi.

Despite the people's cry of outrage to march forth and attack the Gadianton robbers in their strongholds, Commander Gidgiddoni in his wisdom, persuaded the people that the wiser thing to do would be to prepare for war in their own strongholds and on their own turf in the land of Zarahemla and defend themselves there against Giddianhi and his robbers. (3 Nephi 3:)

In the eighteenth year after the signs of Christ's birth, the Gadianton robbers poured out of the hills and took possession of all the lands both in the south and in the north. The Nephite people had abandoned those places to gather in one area for their own defense as ordered by their wise governor. As the robbers spread across the desolate and deserted land, they soon realized that there was no wild game, no livestock, nor food of any kind left behind by the Nephites, which left nothing for them to plunder and no way of feeding themselves. Giddianhi and his robbers refused to farm the land or work in any way to provide for their own subsistence, which left them no alternatives except to attack the Nephites for their provisions, which they proceeded to do during the next year.

As the robber's marched forth out of the hills, and out of their strongholds and their secret places to battle the Nephites, their very appearance with their shaven heads and their lambskin loincloths, which were dyed red in blood, was terribly frightening for any man to look upon. This fearful sight caused the Nephite soldiers to fall to the earth and to cry to the Lord their God to spare them from the awful hordes. The Lord heard their cries and saw their true humility, and he did strengthen them in battle, a battle so terrible and with so much slaughter, that it had no equal since the children of Lehi had come upon the Promised Land. The robber hordes began to fall back against the surprising strength and fierceness of Commander Gidgiddoni's Nephite army. As the robbers fell back towards the borders of the wilderness, Commander Gidgiddoni ordered his men to pursue them without mercy until the wicked Giddianhi and his men were overtaken in their weariness, and Giddianhi, himself, was killed, leaving the Gadianton robbers temporarily without a leader.

The robbers then licked their wounds for two years until another leader, Zemnarihah, took over and deployed his men about the borders of the territory in an attempt to cut the Nephites off from the rest of the land and from gathering provisions. Much to the robbers' disappointment, this plan failed due to the prudent and wise planning of the Nephites and their well-stocked provisions. The robber's blockade was not only a failure, but also their failed economic sanctions and long vigil had caused them to become hungrier by the day. Then to add grief to misery, the Nephite army was conducting guerilla warfare by day and by night against the bedraggled robbers, which was taking a toll upon their numbers.

With little other choice, the stubborn Zemnarihah finally abandoned his siege and commanded his armies to march into the lands northward. Commander Gidgiddoni becoming aware of the plan then deployed many of his men by night into the land northward and then brought the rest of his army up from behind, thereby trapping the armies of Zemnarihah. The Nephites killed hundreds of robbers and took thousands of prisoners, and even Zemnarihah, himself, was captured and hung from a tree. The beaten, weakened, and vanquished Gadianton robbers had come to a great defeat and retreated in haste.

The Nephites singing and praising their God, rejoiced in tears over their victory against the Gadianton robbers. They then did recognize that their great blessing had come about because of their own repentance and humility and because they had called upon the Lord their God for deliverance. (3 Nephi 4:)

The Nephites executed their remaining defiant enemies, but rehabilitated the few repentant robbers who had now become cooperative. These repentant survivors, then had the word of God preached unto them by the Nephites, "And thus they did put an end to all those wicked and secret, and abominable combinations . . ." (3Nephi 5:6) The next four years passed away in peace with an eye single to faith, obedience, gratitude, and the faithful following of the commandments of God.

Twenty-six years after the birth of Christ, the people began to return to the different parts of the land and to those many regions that they had inhabited before. They also granted to the reformed robber Lamanites some land of their own to farm as they now were under a covenant to live in peace.

Commander Gidgiddoni and Governor Lachoneous had established peace throughout the lands of the Nephites, and the people now uninhibited by the violence of war and the plundering of the robbers began to prosper greatly, building new cities and highways, procuring riches, and a great deal of material wealth. By the thirtieth year after Christ's birth, they also had become prideful, boastful, power hungry, and discriminatory against the poor, while they did distinguish themselves by ranks according to their wealth.

In that year, Governor Lachoneous turned the judgment seat over to his son, while lesser judges and lawyers took the law into their own hands and secretly executed "those who testified of the things pertaining to Christ." Even more reprehensible than that, the executions even included some of their own prophets. Obviously, this was strictly against the laws of the land, but the guilty were upheld and supported by their friends through secret covenants, and so they were aided in circumventing justice in spite of their many crimes. These wicked judges, lawyers, and high priest were all in collusion with each other, and they did conspire to rid the country of the chief judge and governor of the land so that they might establish a king over the land in his stead. (3 Nephi 6:)

By the end of the thirtieth year, they had killed the chief judge and destroyed the organized government of the land. The governing authorities were corrupt and the government itself was in complete chaos. For their own survival, the people broke up into separate support groups, tribes and small communities consisting of families and friends, each tribe governing themselves by a chosen leader or chief. The secret combinations also organized into a separate tribe led by a wicked leader called Jacob. They called him their king.

Many prophets had been cast out or stoned to death. Somehow, Nephi the 3rd had escaped this fate and despite his great disappointment and grief over the total corruption and destruction of the government, and the depraved condition of his people, he went among them to testify of Christ and he still attempted to bring them to repentance. He did minister to them with great power and authority, performing miracles, casting out devils and unclean spirits, and he did even miraculously raise his own brother, Timothy, from the dead after he had been stoned to death. (3 Nephi 7:19, 19:4)

Although the majority of the Nephites were angry with Nephi and his perceived self righteous preaching, and his supposed miracles, there were a few who actually believed in his words and therefore were converted and baptized. These were those who had actually been healed by his hand, witnessed his miracles with their own eyes, felt of his great spirit, and saw the great faith that he had in Jesus Christ. (3 Nephi 7:)

In the thirty and third year after Christ's birth, many of the people began to rigorously look for the sign of the three days of darkness that Samuel the Lamanite had prophesied would come at Christ's death. When it did not come, there was much doubt and skepticism, and even disputes over whether it would ever come, or if it was all just a myth. Unfortunately for the non-believers and skeptics, they soon found out that it was not a myth! Nothing would be the same.

In the first month of the next year, a great and terrible storm arose, with thunder and lightning like none that had ever been seen before by the Nephites. The terrible tempest set fire to and destroyed the great city of Zarahemla itself, and the city of Moroni sank into the sea with all its inhabitants, and many other great and notable cities were sunk into the sea, buried under rubble, or burned to the ground. There were great earthquakes that rose up new mountains, sank entire cities, and broke up the highways and byways. This cataclysmic maelstrom from the very bowels of the earth marked no less than the crucifixion and death of the Son of God.

"And there were some who were carried away in the whirlwind; and whither they went no man knoweth, save they know that they were carried away." "And thus the face of the whole earth became deformed, because of the tempest, and the thunderings, and the lightnings, and the quaking of the earth." (3 Nephi 8:16-17)

The great destruction lasted for about three hours and then darkness spread across the land, so thick that no fires, torches, nor candles could be lit, and total darkness pervaded the whole land. There was mourning and howling and weeping as the people declared, "O that we had repented before this great and terrible day . . ." (3 Nephi 8:24)

*　　*　　*

Daniel C. Peterson: "Likewise, the account of the great destruction given in 3 Nephi:8 finds remarkable parallels with what modern seismology and vulcanology show about cataclysmic geological events and with historical reports of such catastrophes. Yet Joseph Smith never saw a volcano and never experienced a significant earthquake, nor is it likely he had read any substantial literature on the subject." Daniel C. Peterson, "Mounting Evidence for the Book of Mormon," Ensign, Jan. 2000

Jeff Lindsay: "Not only is there a location in the Americas where significant volcanic and probably seismic activity occurred near the time specific in the Book of Mormon, but it occurred in the only plausible location for the Book of Mormon based on many other considerations—Mesoamerica. Major lava flows in that area have been dated to about 75 A.D. plus or minus 50 years (one non-LDS scholar, Archaeologist and geologist Payson Sheets, said it was at "about the time of Christ"), making the Book of Mormon account entirely plausible." (see (www.jefflindsay.com/BMEvidences.shtml)

*   *   *

The destruction was devastating, Zarahemla was burned, the city of Moroni was sunk into the sea, the city of Moronihah was buried under the earth, and no city or any part of the land was untouched. The world that the survivors had always known was now totally gone!

Then the voice of Jesus Christ was "heard among all the inhabitants of the earth, upon all the face of this land . . ." The voice declared that he was Alpha and Omega and that the great destruction had come upon the people because of "their wickedness and their abominations" and that he had covered them with earth and destroyed them by fire to hide them from his face, and he declared that this had been done so "that the blood of the prophets and the saints whom I sent among them might not cry unto me from the ground against them." (3 Nephi 9:11)

He also said that he would no longer accept burnt offerings and sacrifices, or the shedding of blood as a sacrifice. He now would only accept "a broken heart and a contrite spirit" in the sincere humility of personal sacrifice. Those who offered that would be baptized "..with fire and with the Holy Ghost . . ." Then he declared that he had "come unto the world to bring redemption unto the world, to save the world from sin." (3 Nephi 9:21)

All the people of the land heard the voice and they were so astounded that there was silence in the land for many hours, until the voice came again saying "O ye people . . . who are of the house of Israel, how oft would I have gathered you as a hen gathered her chickens under her wings . . . and ye would not." This affirmation of a great truth caused the people to weep and howl because of their considerable guilt, and they mourned the lost of their kindred and their friends, and their missing neighbors, and all the rest who were lost to the great destruction.

On the morning of the fourth day, the earth ceased to tremble and groan, and the sun finally swept the darkness away. This caused the wailing and weeping of the people to turn into joy and to give exclamations of humble thanksgiving.

Thus the words of Samuel the Lamanite and the other prophets were fulfilled. The more righteous part of the people was saved from the great destruction, including the righteous Lamanites. Christ had manifested himself to the people and he did ministered to them all with clarity, authority, and a great love for them. (3 Nephi 10:)

3rd Nephi chapters 11 through 26, records the miraculous wonder of Christ's appearance to the people upon this continent and his specific ministry to the righteous people of Nephi on the southern border of the narrow neck of land in the land of Bountiful. As they gathered around the temple, they marveled and spoke of the events of that great and dreadful day. Then suddenly, there was a small but piercing voice that came out of the heavens and introduced the very Son of God to them, the voice calling him his beloved son in whom He was well pleased. Then wonder of wonders and very overwhelming to the multitude that was there, Christ, himself, descended out of the heavens and announced that He was Jesus Christ of whom the prophets had testified. The entire multitude fell to the earth. Christ invited all the righteous to come forth and thrust their hands into his side and actually feel the nail prints in his hands and feet that they each might have a personal witness that He was of whom the prophets had written should come. (3 Nephi 11:12-15)

After many cries of Hosanna from the people, Christ called the prophet Nephi the 3rd out from the multitude to come forth and he said unto him; "I give unto you power that ye shall baptize this people when I am again ascended into heaven."

Can one even imagine what it would actually be like to receive our calling personally from the Savior while we stood face to face with him? Nephi must have been overwhelmed as he was specifically given at that time the authority and the power to baptize in the name of the Son of God by Christ himself. Christ then called others to come forth and He gave them the power to baptize also, giving them specific instructions on the manner of baptism and the exact words that should be pronounced. (3 Nephi 11:18-27)

He then warned them to avoid contention as it was not of him, but of the devil, and He commanded them to go forth to preach repentance and baptism, and to declare his words to the ends of the earth. These twelve special men that Christ had called and gave the power and authority to baptize were the apostles of the remnant of Joseph in the new world.

Stretching his hand out to the multitude, He admonished those present to heed the teachings of the twelve as He had chosen them especially to administer to this people. Finally He spoke to this multitude in the same manner as He had spoken to those people on the other side of the world at the Sermon on the Mount, teaching them the wisdom of the Beatitudes, and commanding them to "be perfect even as I, or your Father who is in heaven is perfect." (3 Nephi 12:48)

Christ admonished the Nephite people to give to the poor and to pray and fast in secret, and not to seek to be praised or seen of men in these things, nor should they seek after riches. He taught them how to pray by giving them the example of "The Lord's Prayer."

Then speaking to the twelve, He said, "Therefore take no thought, saying. what shall we eat? or, What shall we drink? or, Wherewithal shall we be clothed? For your heavenly Father knoweth that ye have need of all these things. But seek ye first the Kingdom of God . . ." (3 Nephi 13:31-33)

Turning back to the multitude, He counseled them to not judge one another, but to do unto others as you would have them do unto you. He advised them to beware of false prophets and to judge people by their fruits, or in other words, not by their lip service but by their good works. He counseled them to build their own houses of faith upon the rock and to not build upon the sand. (3 Nephi 14:)

The Law of Moses is fulfilled in and through Christ and ". . . all things had become new." Then Christ revealed to the twelve that they were the lost sheep that He had spoken of while He was in Jerusalem, and they were the remnant of Joseph who was sold into Egypt. (3 Nephi 15:) Christ declares that He has sheep in other folds not among the Nephites or Lamanites, or in the land of Jerusalem. He also said that He will reveal the truth unto the Gentiles who will scatter and scourge this seed, the house of Israel, this being their judgment, but in the end, Christ will remember his covenant with the house of Israel, including the seed of Lehi, and restore the complete fullness of the gospel to them. (3 Nephi 16:)

After speaking to the Nephites at length, Christ told them to return to their homes, ponder and pray, and prepare for the morrow. As He was getting ready to leave them, He told them, "But now I go unto the Father, and also to show myself unto the lost tribes of Israel, for they are not lost unto the Father, for He knoweth whither He hath taken them." (3 Nephi 17:4)

It is generally believed that the lost tribes of Israel will be the third witness, the third group of people to testify and write scriptural witness to the divinity of Jesus Christ.

As Christ was preparing to leave, He cast his eyes upon the crowd, and He perceived that the people didn't want him to leave them just yet. Having compassion upon them, He told them to bring forth their sick, their lame, their blind and any others afflicted, and at that time with great compassion, He did heal them.

Then bowing down upon the earth, He prayed unto his Father in Heaven in words that cannot be written nor any tongue can speak. He blessed each child among them while angels from heaven came down and administered to the children as they were encircled by fire. There were about two thousand and five hundred men, women, and children, who witnessed all of this, and they bowed at Christ's feet and they worshipped him in tears. One can only imagine what a truly wondrous event this was for these people? (3 Nephi 17:)

Christ then commanded his disciples to bring forth bread and wine, and He asked the multitude to sit upon the ground. He broke the bread, blessed it, and gave it to his disciples, who were then commanded to administer it to the people. In a like manner, He also administered the wine, with that too being served to the multitude with the commandment to do this in a spirit of repentance, obedience to his commandments, and to be a witness unto the Father that they would always remember him. He warned them to not allow the blatantly unworthy to partake of the sacrament, and finally he touched each of the twelve giving them the power to give the Holy Ghost, and then He ascended into heaven. (3 Nephi 18:)

The multitudes returned to their homes for the evening, but with great anticipation and excitement as they talked about Christ appearing again on the morrow. When the next day came, they gathered again with the twelve standing in their midst. The disciples ministered to them and caused them to kneel upon the ground and pray. They then all gathered at the waters edge. "And it came to pass that Nephi went down into the water and was baptized." (3 Nephi 19:11) He then baptized all of the other disciples and they were all fallen upon by the Holy Ghost and encircled by "as if it were fire." As if that was not enough, Christ himself came down and stood among them and commanded that the disciples and the entire multitude should kneel and pray. Going off a little ways by himself, Christ knelt and prayed to his Father thanking Him for giving the Holy Ghost to the disciples and asking that it be given to all those who would believe in their words. (3 Nephi 19:)

He then came forward and administered the sacrament to the twelve and afterwards commanded that they should administer the sacrament to the multitudes. Even though no bread or wine had been brought by any of them, all were miraculously able to take the sacrament and be filled with the spirit.

Reminding them that they were the remnant of the house of Israel, He said that He would fulfill the covenant that He had made with Abraham and Jacob and the house of Israel, even though the Gentiles would scourge the people of this land for a while. The Gentiles would be set up as a free people in this free land by the power of the Father so that they could bring the word of God to this remnant of Jacob, the descendants of Father Lehi.

Grave warnings were given to the Gentiles. If they are not obedient to the Lord's commandments and are not repentant, the Lord will "execute vengeance and fury upon them", but if they believe in Christ and are repentant, He will establish his church among them and they will assist in gathering the remnant of Jacob and house of Israel. (3 Nephi 21:21-22)

Christ quotes Isaiah and admonishes the people to study this great prophet's words, as they are great, and also to search the words of the other prophets. He then commands Nephi the 3rd to bring forth the records. After casting his eyes upon the plates, Christ gently chastises Nephi and the other disciples for not keeping the records up to date, particularly by not writing down the words and the testimony of Samuel the Lamanite. (3 Nephi 23:7-13)

He reminds them to not rob God in their tithes and offerings so that God can open the windows of heaven with great blessings while He rebukes "the devourer" that he shall not destroy the fruits of the ground.

He quotes the prophet Malachi, emphasizing that Elijah the prophet will "turn the heart of the fathers to the children and the heart of the children to their fathers." (see 3 Nephi chapters 20-25)

Speaking of Malachi, Christ said "These scriptures, which ye had not with you, the Father commanded that I should give unto you, for it was wisdom in him that they should be given unto future generations." (3 Nephi 26:2)

This statement makes sense, since the prophet Malachi lived and prophesied after Lehi and his family had left Jerusalem and therefore his writings were not on the brass plates that Lehi and his sons had brought across the great waters, and so they had not his words.

In 3 Nephi chapter 26, Mormon who is editing and compiling the records of Nephi, acknowledges that not "even a hundredth part of the things which Jesus did truly teach unto the people" can be written in this book. He also said that the Lord forbade him from writing all that was engraved upon the plates of Nephi. He then testifies that the Lord did truly show himself to these people, and He taught them for the space of three days, and he taught them great and marvelous things, things that cannot be written by any man. (3 Nephi 26:)

At one point, while the disciples were journeying, preaching, and baptizing, they were united in fasting and prayer when Christ came and stood in their midst. They told him that there were some disputes among the people as to what the church should be called. Christ told them that if it be Moses' church then call it by Moses' name, "but if it be called in my name then it is my church." Christ made it quite clear that every thing they should do, should be done in his name, including the naming of his church, therefore it should be called The Church of Jesus Christ. He then told them that what ever they should ask the Father in his name, would be given to them. (3 Nephi 27:)

He also asked each of them, what they would desire of him after He returned to his Father in Heaven. Nine of the disciples asked that they be allowed to come dwell with him in Heaven, after their ministry here on earth was finished. He granted their request, saying that at age seventy-two, they would come unto him in his Kingdom and find rest and then dwell with him there.

The other three disciples were reluctant to tell Christ what they wished, but He perceived what they desired and He told them that He knew that they wanted to be like John the beloved and never taste death. Because they desired to bring the souls of men to Christ as long as mortal men existed, they would be greatly blessed and never experience pain, and never die in the manner of men, but they would be changed in a twinkling of an eye to immortality when the Savior came again in all his glory.

After telling the disciples that "the Holy Ghost beareth record of the Father and me, and the father giveth the Holy Ghost unto the children of men, because of me", He then touched each of the disciples with his finger, except the three, and departed from them.

Mormon writes that he, himself, was forbidden to give the names of the three transfigured Nephite disciples, but that he had personally seen them and they had ministered to him face to face. He says that he knows not "whether they were mortal or immortal, from the day of their transfiguration" but he knows that they went upon the face of the land ministering and baptizing, and were thrown into prisons, deep pits, and dens of wild beast, but were never harmed as "the powers of the earth could not hold them." He also writes that the three will be among the Gentiles and the Jews but the people will not know them, and they will bring about great and marvelous works before the great judgment day. (3 Nephi 28:)

*   *   *

Bruce R. McConkie, Mormon Doctrine, p.793 THREE NEPHITES

"They were to be free from pain and sorrow (except for the sins of the world), and were to minister, "as the angels of God," unto the Jews, Gentiles, scattered tribes of Israel, "and unto all nations, kindreds, tongues, and people." (3 Ne. 28.) They continued their ministry among the Nephites for some 300 years, until the time of Mormon, when they were finally withdrawn because of the wickedness of the people. (4 Ne. 30-37; Morm. 1:13-16.) Unbeknownst to the world, they are continuing their assigned ministry at this time, and there have been occasions when they have appeared to members of the Church in this final dispensation. It is the common practice in the Church to call them the Three Nephites." Bruce R. McConkie

Encyclopedia of Mormonism: "Latter-day Saint scriptures speak of a unique class of beings, persons whom the Lord has "translated" or changed from a mortal state to one in which they are temporarily not subject to death, and in which they experience neither pain nor sorrow except for the sins of the world. Translation is a necessary condition in special instances to further the work of the Lord. Translated beings are not resurrected beings, though all translated beings either have since been or yet will be resurrected or "changed in the twinkling of an eye" to a resurrected state (3 Ne. 28:8). The scriptures do not define differences between transfiguration and translation, but it appears that transfiguration is more temporary, as in Matthew 17:1-9 and Moses 1:11, occurring primarily to permit one to behold spiritual things not possible in the mortal condition." Encyclopedia of Mormonism, Vol.4, TRANSLATED BEINGS

*   *   *

Mormon writes in the last chapters of third Nephi that when "these sayings" shall come unto the Gentiles, then we will know that the covenant that the Lord made with the children of Israel "concerning their restoration to the lands of their inheritance" will be fulfilled and is being fulfilled. In other words, when the book of Mormon comes forth among the Gentiles in America, the people shall know that the Lord is fulfilling his covenant with the House of Israel and is gathering them from the four corners of the earth.

All people are warned against spurning the Jew or any of the remnants of the House of Israel. In the modern world, there are many nations who seek the destruction of Israel. The book of Zechariah chapter 12, in the Old Testament, speaks of the last days and the final Great War, which will engage all nations at Jerusalem. This will eventually lead to a great battle where the Lord will defend Israel and He will "destroy all nations that come against Jerusalem." Also, the unbelievers and false witnesses are warned, "Wo unto him that shall deny the revelations of the Lord," saying falsely that the Lord no longer works through revelation or prophesy, or the gifts of the Holy Ghost. (3 Nephi 29:)

The Gentiles are commanded to turn away from all manner of wickedness, repent, and be baptized in Christ's name for the remission of their sins, and then they will be numbered with the house of Israel. (3 Nephi 30:)

Mormon's abridgement of Third Nephi, which recounts the personal appearance and the sacred words and acts of Jesus Christ, is some of the most touching and inspiring chapters of the entire Book of Mormon. Many members of the church have found these verses to be the most glorifying of all scripture and have even called the book of Third Nephi, the fifth gospel, indicating its great standing and importance along side of Mathew, Mark, Luke, and John.

*   *   *

"It is clear that Third Nephi contains some of the most moving and powerful passages in all scripture. Third Nephi is a book that should be read and read again. Its testimony of the resurrected Christ in America is given in purity and beauty." Teachings of Ezra Taft Benson, p.60 (CR April 1987, Ensign 17 [May 1987]: 4, 6.)

*   *   *

CHAPTER SEVENTEEN

* * *

THE DAYS AFTER CHRIST HAD RISEN

By the thirty and sixth year after Christ's birth, only a few short years after He had walked among them, the disciples of Jesus had established his church among all the people and had converted and baptized all of the Nephites and all of Lamanites, "upon all the face of the land." There was peace and justice through out the land and there was no contention among them. Apparently the people were living a type of "United order." The Book of Mormon describes it so; "And they had all things common among them, therefore there were no rich and poor, bond and free, but they were all made free . . ." (4 Nephi 1:3)

The twelve disciples went among the people preaching and performing many marvelous works and miracles, even healing the blind and raising the dead, while the people prospered and rebuilt their cities, even the great city of Zarahemla, which had been burnt to the ground. They multiplied greatly in their numbers and became "an exceedingly fair and delightsome people." By the hundredth year after Christ's birth, all the disciples, except "the three who should tarry", had passed away including Nephi the 3rd, and new disciples had been ordained in their place. The son of Nephi the 3rd was also called Nephi. This Nephi the 4th had now taken over the care and writing of the sacred records. The people were at complete peace with each other and lived as one people with no designation of Lamanites or Nephites, "nor any manner of-ites", just one united people living in happiness. This of course, was an extremely rare occurrence among the Nephites and Lamanites, and for that matter among human beans in general.

In the hundred and tenth year after Christ's birth, all the first generation who had seen and heard and been taught by Christ, had all passed away, never-the-less there still remained peace and prosperity among the people.

Nephi the 4th, a righteous man who had inherited the calling as a sacred record keeper, also passed away after having passed the plates of Nephi on to his son, Amos the 1st. He had charged his son with the sacred obligation to preserve, protect, and to write upon the sacred records. This Amos the 1st then was obedient to his father and his God, and he dutifully protected and kept the records for another eighty-four years.

Then in the hundred and ninety-fourth year after Christ's birth, he too, having anticipated the end of his days, passed the sacred records on to one of his sons before he went "the way of all the earth." His son, Amos the 2nd, now following in his father's footsteps, continued to keep, protect, and write upon the plates of Nephi, and so the long legacy of keeping and protecting the sacred records continued.

Death is just a part of God's much bigger plan and it exempts no man, no matter his standing with the Lord. We must all accept that even when it's a loved one. Meanwhile, those that are left behind must continue on in one way or another in their mortal journey, whether that be for good or for bad, even as they use up their valuable time here on this earth. Eventually we will all be judged for how we used up our precious mortal time here on earth, which may some day cause considerable anxiety for some. And so it was for the Nephites living two centuries after Christ's death, as the cycles of life and death, and good and evil carried on relentlessly.

Among the Nephites, there was still a general peace throughout the land, even a couple of hundred years after Christ came to the people, but there eventually came among them those who would revolt against the church and they began to call themselves Lamanites. Two hundred and one years after Christ's birth, the people were greatly prospering and they began to be caught up in the pride of their riches, their costly apparel, and their fine jewelry, and they began to divide into different social classes accordingly. In this environment, the true Church of Christ was no longer serving the desires and purposes of the greedy ones who strayed from the straight and narrow path as they established many new and drastically different churches, all on crooked paths as the calendar turned over to 210 A.D. These Churches were designed to meet their personal materialistic needs, and to prop them up in their pride while showing off their wealth and their high station in the community, as they only professed their belief in Christ. "Yet they did deny the more parts of his gospel . . ." (4 Nephi 1:27)

There began to be a persecution of the followers of the true church, including even the harassment of the three special disciples of Jesus who continued to tarry on the earth among the people. After casting these Three Nephites into prison, the wicked were shocked to see the prison walls twist and fall to the ground due to the power of God within the three. Never the less, instead of being awed, the people hardened their hearts and cast the three disciples into a furnace of fire. When that cruel act was also found to be wanting in the disposing of the disciples, the wicked ones then proceeded to throw the disciples "into the dens of wild beast" wherein the three Nephite disciples played with the beasts as if they were lambs and they miraculously emerged unharmed.

The wicked were of such hardened hearts, that they completely ignored the unbelievable miracles that they had seen with their own two eyes, and would not even acknowledge them as being miracles. Subsequently, being influenced by corrupt priest and false prophets, they did continue to smite and abuse all of the people who followed and believed in Jesus Christ.

In the two hundredth and thirty first year after Christ's birth, there was a great divide among the people, with the righteous being called Nephites, Jacobites, Josephites, and Zoramites. On the other hand, those who rejected Christ and dwindled in unbelief were called Lamanites, Lemuelites, and Ishmaelites, and they willfully rebelled against the gospel of Jesus Christ. Alas, the wicked were greater in numbers than the righteous and they did teach their children to actually hate the people of God. Thus being so corrupt, they once again began to build up their secret combinations and began to spew out their vile oaths in the same wicked tradition of the once annihilated Gadianton robbers.

Unfortunately and in a very disappointing way, even the so-called people of God, the ones who were called the people of Nephi, the ones who should know better, became puffed up in the pride of their riches and began to drift into unrighteousness. And it became very evident that this great prosperity in itself did and without warning, absolutely taint, skew, and weaken the spirituality of even the righteous ones of the Nephites.

Certainly there must be a lesson in this for us, and we would be foolish to not learn from these things. Expensive clothes, large homes, and fine automobiles can be a very seductive temptation to bolster our personal self-image and cause us to appear to be a success among our peers. Then there is that subtle insidious worldly desire to be highly thought of among our friends, neighbors, co-workers, and our fellow church members. When the material things of this world are high on our priority list, just as it was among the Nephites, our spirituality almost always suffers, and it is vital that we are reminded of this truth in our personal lives and use this knowledge. Yes of course, we must be in the world, but hopefully not of the world. (4Nephi 1:43)

By the end of the three hundred years after Christ's birth, all the people, both Nephites and Lamanites and all the other "ites", had become exceedingly wicked and caught up in the love of their silver and their gold and all manner of wickedness, and they built up churches unto themselves, and once again they began to deal in the secret oaths and the combinations of the Gadianton robbers. Understandably the disciples of Jesus did sorrow greatly.

In 305 A.D., the sacred records once again changed hands, as the responsibility of keeping them safe weighed up on another sacred record keeper. So Amos the 2nd, grandson of Nephi the fourth, delivered to his own brother Ammaron, that most sacred assignment of keeping and protecting the records of Nephi, and then he too passed on to the great hereafter.

Sixteen years later, in 321 A.D., being constrained by the spirit of the Holy Ghost, this Ammaron, the son of Amos the 1st, brother to Amos the 2nd, and grandson of Nephi the 4th, did bury the sacred records, "yea, even all the sacred records which had been handed down from generation to generation", and he buried them in the Hill called Shim. He hid them unto the Lord that they might come forth at another time; that exact time period being in the Lord's own good time and in the Lord's own good wisdom for the benefit of the remnant of the house of Jacob, and this in turn fulfilling the promises of the Lord. (4 Nephi chapter 1:)

*   *   *

THREE IMPORTANT HILLS

In the first chapter of Mormon, the prophet Mormon reveals that he was sent to the hill called Shim in the land of Antum by his mentor Ammaron, to retrieve the sacred records when he was twenty-four years old. This was the hill where Ammaron had previously been inspired to bury the plates for safekeeping to wait for the hand of Mormon. (Mormon 1:3)

Apparently, the hill Shim was not as well suited for hiding the sacred plates as the Hill Cumorah. Mormon 4:23 states: "And now I, Mormon, seeing that the Lamanites were about to over throw the land, therefore I did go to the hill Shim, and did take up all the records which Ammaron had hid up unto the Lord." Mormon must have felt that there was a safer place for the sacred records to be kept.

Ether 9:3 tell us that the Jaredite King Omer and his family, in their flight to safety, passed by the hill of Shim and the hill where all the Nephites were destroyed. We know the hill where all the Nephites were destroyed, to be the hill Cumorah from our reading in Mormon chapter 6:2-6, which plainly tells us that this hill was where the Lamanites and Nephites all gathered for the last battle and was called the hill Cumorah. Both the hill Shim and the hill Cumorah apparently were in the same general area north of the narrow neck of land. These same verses tell us that Cumorah was also the hill where Mormon buried the plates to keep them safe from the Lamanites. Then Ether 15:11 tells us that the hill Ramah, where all the Jaredites were destroyed when they met in their last battle, is the same hill where Moroni's father, Mormon, had buried the plates. Therefore by comparing the statements used in these verses, we must logically conclude from these scriptures that the hill Ramah and the hill Cumorah are one in the same hill.

Thus this infamous and very important historic hill was the very site of the final destruction of two civilizations; two stubborn civilizations that apparently in their great deafness ignored their prophets and those very clear warnings from the Lord, as well as his immutable justice and his unchangeable commandments.

Lastly, this very hill was also a most important sacred depository for very significant historical records written on the sacred metal plates. These plates contained the prophetic words and wisdom of many ancient prophets whose stewardships were spread over a thousand years. Metaphorically, it could be said of this hill, that it is the womb and the birthplace of some of the most correct and valuable scriptures that have thus been revealed to us.

There is one other interesting side note that comes to light about this particular area around the hill Cumorah. It relates to the Mulekites, or more accurately, the people of Zarahemla, as they are referred to in Alma.

*   *   *

Encyclopedia of Mormonism, Vol.1, CUMORAH
"Cumorah had also been the site of the destruction of the Jaredites roughly 900 years earlier. Moroni states in the book of Ether that the Jaredites gathered for battle near "the hill Ramah," the same hill

where his father, Mormon, hid up "the records unto the Lord, which were sacred" (Ether 15:11). It was near the first landing site of the people of Mulek (Alma 22:30), just north of the land Bountiful and a narrow neck of land (Alma 22:32)."

*   *   *

We indicated earlier in this book that the Mulekites had landed in the middle lands between the northern landing of the Jaredites and the southern landing of Father Lehi's family. It is well established, that the great city of Zarahemla, which was founded by the Mulekites, was south of the land of Desolation, and even somewhat south of the Land of Bountiful, but yet was north of the Land of Lehi-Nephi, and therefore unquestionably located in the middle between these two regions. Yet, this verse in Alma 22:30 "..discovered by the people of Zarahemla, it being the place of their first landing" seems to indicate that although the Mulekites had eventually settled in the middle lands, the actual original landing of the people of Zarahemla, or the Mulekites, may have been much farther north in the "land northward", being much closer to the area where the Jaredites originally had landed and settled.

All of the doings and pursuits of the Jaredites took place in the "land northward", including the great battle at the hill Ramah, which would later be known as the hill Cumorah among the Nephites. Although there is certainly no definitive evidence as to just where Ramah or Hill Cumorah was located, Book of Mormon researchers have come up with some clues out of the Book of Mormon that might give us a better idea.

"In 1981, Palmer identified 13 geographical conditions required for the Book of Mormon Hill Ramah/Cumorah:

1. near eastern seacoast
2. near narrow neck of land
3. on a coastal plain and near other mountains and valleys
4. one day's journey south of a large body of water
5. an area of many rivers and waters
6. presence of fountains (possibly waterfalls)
7. water gives military advantage
8. an escape route southward
9. hill large enough to view hundreds of thousands of bodies
10. hill must be a significant landmark
11. hill must be free standing so people can camp around it
12. in temperate climate with no cold or snow
13. in a volcanic zone susceptible to earthquakes"
    (See www.jefflindsay.com/BMEvidences.shtlm)

* * *

All the above requirements would indicate that the Hill Ramah and the Hill Cumorah, which by logic are the same hill, are probably not the same hill as Joseph Smith's Hill Cumorah located in New York State, which may have possibly been given that name as an honorary title after the original hill in the Book of Mormon. This is unquestionably just speculation that there are two Hill Cumorahs, even though it is consistent with there being two different Bountifuls and two different cities called Jerusalem. Never the less, a great deal of circumstantial evidence would suggest that there are two Hill Cumorahs. See more about these evidences in Chapter twenty of this book.

* * *

CHAPTER EIGHTEEN

* * *

MORMON, COMMANDER OF THE NEPHITES

Shortly after Ammaron, the grandson of Nephi the 4th, buried the plates in the hill Shim, he approached a young ten-year-old boy who was called by the name of Mormon. The young man was named after his father, and a proud descendant of Nephi the 1st. This young boy Mormon had been taught in the ways of the learning of his people and was as Ammaron called him, a sober child who was quick to observe. Being impressed by the young man and probably inspired to do so, Ammaron chose Mormon to succeed himself as the keeper of the sacred records. He told the boy Mormon that when he should reach the age of twenty-four years old, that he should go to the land of Antum to a hill called Shim and recover the plates of Nephi, leaving the other plates hidden in the hill. Then he told the young man that he should write upon the plates of Nephi all things that he had observed concerning this people.

A year later, Mormon was taken by his father to the land of Zarahemla where the whole of the land had become covered with buildings and the people were "as numerous almost, as it were the sand of the sea." A war had begun between the two renewed groups of opposition, and so it came to pass that the waters of the Sidon River became the confluence for the Nephites and the Lamanites to do battle. With numbers exceeding thirty thousand men, the Nephites were able to defeat the Lamanites once again to bring peace to the people and upon all the land round about for approximately the next four years.

Unfortunately, both groups of opposition, that is the Nephites and the Lamanites, continued to carry on unrepentant in all their wickedness. The people of the land had become so wayward and so blatantly evil that the Lord in His great wisdom was compelled to completely remove the three Nephite disciples from among the people, and thus remove the healing powers of the priesthood, as the well the giving of the Holy Ghost. (Mormon 1:13-14) What a very sad commentary on the moral condition of the people of that time period. Do we as a society now find ourselves approaching such deplorable conditions in our times? How far away is it?

At age fifteen, Mormon having been visited by the Lord and having gained a testimony of Jesus Christ, had attempted to preach to his own wayward people and bring them back to the straight and narrow, but to no avail. The Lord then forbade him to preach to them at all. Their overall morality and sense of decency degenerated by the day as they entertained sorcery, witchcraft, magic and other abominations, and they willfully rebelled against their God. Once again, there began to be many battles between the Nephites and the Lamanites, and so death and great violence was spread upon the land once more.

Apparently the young boy Mormon, in his sixteenth year, was very mature physically and mentally, well beyond his youthful years, and he must have exhibited apparent outstanding leadership qualities too, as he was chosen by the people of Nephi to command their armies. This point in time was 326 years since the birth of Christ, and the young Chief Captain Mormon, at the tender age of sixteen, now found himself with the very heavy responsibility of being the Chief Commander of all the Nephite armies. (Mormon 2:)

Despite his men being frightened by the powerful onslaught of the Lamanite warriors and actually being driven from several Nephite cities, the young Commander Mormon was able to rally his men and finally lead them to a great victory over King Aaron and his 44,000 Lamanites in the year 331 A.D. At this point, the Nephites had begun to repent of their grievous sins, but much to Mormon's disappointment, their humbling attitude seemed to be more due to the trials placed upon them by the Lamanites and Gadianton robbers than to their sincere faith and allegiance to Christ.

By the three hundred and forty-fifth year, the people were so wicked that they were no longer protected by the Lord, and so now were being driven from place to place by the relentless pursuit of the Lamanites. Mormon mourned over their dumbfounding stubbornness and their rebellion against their God saying that "the day of grace was passed" not only temporally but spiritually too. He watched as thousands were hewn down and "heaped up as dung upon the face of the land." They finally found temporary safety in the land of Jashon, which was near where Mormon's old mentor, Ammaron, had buried the sacred plates in the northland. At this time, Mormon did retrieve the plates and began recording his own record upon the plates of Nephi, just as he had been instructed to do so by Ammaron many years before.

In the next few years, the people of Nephi were driven from Jashon northward to the land of Shem. There they fortified the city of Shem, while Captain Mormon fortified his men with the power of "great spiritual energy" causing them to stand firm in boldness and confidence, and as such, his 30,000 soldiers were able to miraculously defeat 50,000 Lamanites.

In the three hundred and fiftieth year, the people of Nephi made a treaty with the Lamanites and also the Gadianton robbers. This treaty reserved all the land north of the narrow neck of land for the possession of the Nephites, while the Lamanites would control all the land to the south, thus bringing peace to the land for a while. (Mormon 2:)

Ten years later, the Lamanites renewed their long-standing hatred and grievances against the Nephites and prepared for battle in their obsession to destroy the Nephite people. The Lord commanded Mormon to cry repentance to his people, which he did, but once again in vain. Mormon then caused that the people be gathered together in the north in the land of Desolation; and so they gathered in a city that was by a narrow pass leading to the land southward. Here they were able to fend off several attacks by the armies of the Lamanites during the next couple of years, driving them back into their own lands, which inspired the people of Nephi to boast in their own strength and skills as great warriors. Unfortunately, they had become so very wicked, that Commander Mormon refused to lead them into battle, and stood by as an "idle witness" to their boastful unrepentant wickedness and gross abominations. (Mormon 3:)

"It is by the wicked that the wicked are punished" and so it was that the judgments of God came upon the unrepentant Nephites. They were driven out of the city of Desolation to the nearby seashore city of Teancum and then attacked there also. When they repelled that attack successfully, they boasted in their own strength and retook the city of Desolation, and they delighted in all the violence and the bloodshed. Startling as it may sound, even in the face of many thousands of men on both sides being slain for no more reason than the absolute profanity of seeing how much bloodshed and violence they could wreak upon each other, they continued as if it were an addiction to the blood and the slaughter of their enemies. This blood and horror had become an attraction of its own merit, like it was an obsession far beyond the supposed defense of their own families and lands.

The Nephite victories were short lived as the massive Lamanite armies struck the city of Desolation once again, as well as the city of Teancum. Capturing many women and children, the Lamanites warriors being completely void now of any compassion whatsoever, made blood sacrifices of their innocent victims to their idols and Gods. The Nephites were swept before their enemies "as a dew before the sun" resulting in a great slaughter of the Nephite people. On seeing this, Captain Mormon went to the hill Shim where his mentor Ammaron had buried the plates. There he retrieved all of the sacred records, including the ones he had been instructed to not touch before, and took them unto himself, very much determined to preserve them. (Mormon 4:)

The Lamanites continued their attacks, while the wearied and beaten Nephites looked to Commander Mormon to save them from destruction. Finally unable to withhold his compassion from them any longer, he gave into their request and once again led them into battle, even though he knew that it was a lost cause, as the Lord could not save the Nephites now due to their unwillingness to repent of their great iniquities. Mormon had little hope for the outcome, but never the less with his able leadership they were able to maintain the security of several Nephite cities, even though the outlying villages and towns were burned and destroyed by the Lamanites.

By 385 A.D., the large hordes of Lamanites warriors had killed or scattered all of the Nephites; the slow were dead and the swift took flight to a temporary safety only. Mormon said that the carnage was so terrible that he could not describe it, but that he must record what he could so that it might be a warning and a lesson to the remnants of the house of Israel and to the Gentiles. The remnant of this people would "become a dark, a filthy, and a loathsome people," scattered, mistreated, and disrespected by the Gentile, but in the end, the Gentiles would bring back the gospel to the surviving descendants of the Lamanites, these descendants being the remnant of the house of Israel that Lord had promised that he would preserve. (Mormon 5:)

Seeing that the end of his people was near and that it was unlikely that they could hold out much longer, Commander Mormon wrote a letter to the commander and King of the Lamanites and asked him to allow the Nephites to gather at the hill Cumorah in the land of "many waters, rivers, and fountains." There the Nephites would meet the Lamanites in pitch battle, a great and final battle to end all battles. The Lamanite King agreed and did let the all the Nephites gather in the land of Cumorah and pitch their tents surrounding the Hill Cumorah to wait for the last great conflict with the Lamanites.

Mormon then feeling his age, and oh so very tired, and having been commanded by the Lord to not allow the sacred records to fall into the hands of the Lamanites, took the sacred records and buried them in the hill Cumorah, except for the few records which he would pass on to his son, Moroni the 2nd.

When the final and great battle began, the Lamanites in great hordes fell upon the terrified Nephites with sword and all manner of weapons bringing them to the edge of a virtual annihilation. Enumerating the fallen, General Mormon said that he lost 10,000 men and then goes on to name another dozen Nephite commanders along with his son Commander Moroni, who also lost 10,000 men each, all hewn down and slaughtered. He then said that there were another ten commanders with 10,000 each who also fell and were destroyed. This all calculates out to around two hundred and thirty thousand men who were slaughtered altogether among the Nephites. Apparently, even these staggering numbers among the Nephite soldiers were greatly overshadowed by what must have been an absolutely massive number of savage and murderous Lamanite warriors in full attack.

The Nephites as a people were virtually exterminated; although Mormon does mention that there were some who did escape into the south countries and a few more who deserted to the Lamanite camps leaving a small remnant of the Nephite people to be mixed with and assimilated into the Lamanite people. The few Nephites who would survive the destruction would intermingle with the Lamanites fulfilling the promise to Joseph who was sold into Egypt that "thy seed shall not utterly be destroyed."

Thus there remained only twenty-four souls left standing with General Mormon, and significantly including his own son Moroni the 2nd. Mormon touches our heart strings when he mourns the great destruction of his people saying; "O ye fair sons and daughters, ye fathers and mothers, ye husbands and wives, ye fair ones, how is it that ye could have fallen! But behold, ye are gone, and my sorrow cannot bring your return." (Mormon 6:19-20)

Can we as a society and individuals glean any wisdom from the sad tale of such a stubborn and foolish people, or should we just resign ourselves to the fact that history repeats itself and the foibles of human nature will probably never change?

*   *   *

Encyclopedia of Mormonism

"As general of the Nephite armies (Morm. 2-6), Mormon helped to preserve his people from destruction by the Lamanites for some fifty-eight years, but then began to lose them first to sin and then to death (Morm. 2:11-15). Even so, he taught survivors that they would be spared if they would repent and obey the gospel of Jesus Christ, "but it was in vain; and they did not realize that it was the Lord that had spared them, and granted unto them a chance for repentance" (3:3). At one time the Nephites became so vicious and hardened that Mormon refused to lead them into battle (3:11). But he could not bear to watch them perish, and although he had no hope that they could survive, he relented (5:1) and led them into their last battle from which only he, his son Moroni, and a few others survived (8:2-3). Moroni lived to complete his father's record (8:1)." Encyclopedia of Mormonism, Vol.2, MORMON

*   *   *

Commander Mormon's soul was "rent with anguish" over the slain of his people and he lamented "O that ye had repented before this great destruction had come upon you." Talking to the dead, he says, "The eternal Father of heaven knowth your state; and he doth with you according to his justice and mercy." (Mormon 6:22)

He then turns his thoughts to the remnant of this fallen people and their future posterity, implying that God will see to it that they will have his words. In Mormon Chapter 7, Commander Mormon writes his final words reminding the descendants of the Lamanites of their great heritage; "Know ye that ye are of the house of Israel."

(Mormon 7:2) "Know ye that ye must come to the knowledge of your fathers, and repent of all your sins and iniquities and believe in Jesus Christ, that he is the son of God, and that he was slain by the Jews, and by the power of the father he hath risen again whereby he hath gained the victory over the grave; and also in him is the sting of death swallowed up." (Mormon 7:5)

He admonishes them, warns them, and invites them to repent and be baptized and to accept the Gospel of Christ. He emphasizes the divinity and purpose of Jesus Christ and the necessity of repentance and baptism in order to dwell in the presence of God.

He makes reference to the Bible and the Book of Mormon, which will come by way of the Gentiles to this remnant of the house of Jacob, "the people of the first covenant." Finally, he concludes all his writing with the promise that if they are baptized with water and fire and the Holy Ghost, as the Savior commands, "it shall be well with you in the Day of Judgment. Amen." (Mormon 7:10)

*   *   *

"Mormon was a prophet, an author, and the last Nephite military commander (c. A.D. 310-385). The Book of Mormon bears his name because he was the major abridger-writer of the gold plates from which it was translated. He was prepared by the experiences of his youth to become a prophet: he was taught "the learning of [his] people," was a "sober child" and "quick to observe," and in his fifteenth year was "visited of the Lord". At sixteen he became the general of all the Nephite armies and largely succeeded in preserving his people from destruction until A.D. 385, when virtually all of them but his son Moroni 2 were destroyed in battles with the Lamanites. As keeper of the Nephite records, Mormon abridged the large plates of Nephi, bound with them the small plates of Nephi, and added his own short history. Before his death, he hid the records entrusted to him in the hill Cumorah, 'save it were these few plates which I gave unto my son Moroni.'" Encyclopedia of Mormonism, Vol.2, MORMON

*   *   *

General Mormon was an exceptional leader and military officer by any one's standards. He is one more outstanding hero in a long line of Book of Mormon heroes, and without question there is something here for us to admire and to learn from, and to hold up as a worthy example to our youth. Moroni 8:10-11 indicates that Mormon and his son Moroni were both "ministered to" by the three Nephites, giving us an indication of their good standing with the Lord. Mormon is most certainly a great example of the persistence of the faithful standing strong even when the majority of the people around him were heading down the wrong path to their own destruction. Despite the very sad and disappointing ending for him and his people at the conclusion of his mortal life, we don't have to wonder about his personal glory and reward in the afterlife and his secure standing with the Lord.

*   *   *

CHAPTER NINETEEN

* * *

MORONI, THE LAST PROPHET OF THE NEPHITES

Moroni the 2nd, son of Commander Mormon, was a man of faith and a man who was obedient to the Lord and to his father. Having been commanded by his father Mormon to do so, he proceeded to write and finish his father's records, and so it was that Moroni himself wrote Mormon chapters eight and nine in our current Book of Mormon. He wrote in the records that the few Nephites that had escaped from the great battle of Cumorah to the land southward were eventually hunted down by the Lamanites and summarily executed. Sadly, his own beloved father Mormon was also executed, along with the very last of all of Nephite warriors and all that stood with him. The mighty Nephite people as a civilization had been exterminated.

In reading Mormon Chapter 8, we read some of the most poignant verses in the entire Book of Mormon. With a pervasive air of hopelessness and despair that reaches through time for more than 1600 years into the future, it plucks strongly at our emotions, even to the heart of our very own personal feelings. Moroni writes these words . . .

Mormon 8:3 "And my father also was killed by them, and I even remain alone to write the sad tale of the destruction of my people. But behold, they are gone, and I fulfill the commandment of my father. And whether they will slay me, I know not."

4 "Therefore I will write and hide up the records in the earth; and whither I go it mattereth not.

5 "Behold, my father hath made this record, and he hath written the intent thereof. And behold, I would write it also if I had room upon the plates, but I have not; and ore I have none, for I am alone. My father hath been slain in battle, and all my kinsfolk, and I have not friends nor whither to go; and how long the Lord will suffer that I may live I know not."

6 "And behold, the Lamanites have hunted my people, the Nephites, down from city to city and from place to place, even until they are no more; and great has been their fall; yea, great and marvelous is the destruction of my people, the Nephites." Mormon 8:3-6

*　　*　　*

There cannot be a more powerful lesson to be learned from these verses; than that the fall of great civilizations comes about through the disobedience of the people of that civilization to God's commandments. This is the same profound warning that is repeated time after time, civilization after civilization, throughout the Book of Mormon. It is a shame that those who need to listen to this warning the most are the same ones on which it is the most wasted, because they will not listen or see the futility of their own blindness, stubbornness, disobedience, and ignorance, and that will invariably doom their societies. Moroni indicates that all the carnage and destruction that came about is by "the hand of the Lord" for justice cannot be denied, and this sad end was brought upon his people through their own doing. (Mormon 8:8)

The Lamanites and the robbers were all that remained alive upon the land and they continued to fight making war and waging carnage even amongst themselves. What is the great truth and lesson here? Civilizations that ignore the Lord's commandments will eventually self-destruct. If the leaders and their people as one disregard God's commandments, they will invariably bring great sorrow upon themselves, their families, and their society, and they will without fail reap the just rewards that will bring to pass their own demise.

Moroni then speaks to us in our day, saying, "Behold, I speak unto you as if ye were present, and yet yea are not. But behold, Jesus Christ hath shown you unto me, and I know your doing." (Mormon 8:35)

Moroni the 2nd saw our day and age, such as it was, and he saw the same disappointing and sobering view that was in the assessment of one of our modern day prophets.

*   *   *

Ezra Taft Benson: "I say to you with all the fervor of my soul: We are sowing the seeds of our own destruction in America and much of the free world today. It is my sober warning to you today that if the trends of the past continue, we will lose that which is as priceless as life itself—our freedom, our liberty, our right to act as free men. It can happen here. It is happening here." Teachings of Ezra Taft Benson, p.582

*   *   *

What did Moroni see in the future concerning our day and age? He saw and prophesied of the coming forth of the Book of Mormon in a day when churches shall be defiled and lifted up in their pride, in a day of great pollutions upon the earth, and there will be wars and rumors of war, and there shall be all manner of whoredoms and abominations. He warns those who would oppose the work of the lord, and then he makes it clear that the eternal purposes of the Lord "shall roll on" despite all obstacles and all opposition. (Mormon 8:26-34)

In the last Chapter of Mormon, Moroni speaks to those who do not believe in Christ, saying that they would be much more comfortable in Hell, than trying to dwell in the Holy presence of a just God as they will be constantly mindful of all their own guilt, filthiness, and misery. He emphasizes that all men will be redeemed from the endless sleep because of the atoning death of Christ and they shall stand before the judgment bar. Warning those who would deny revelations and prophesies, he makes it clear that God does not change and does not cease to be a God of miracles. If miracles seemed to have ceased, it is because of the unbelief of the children of men. He emphasizes that; "And he that believeth and is baptized shall be saved, but he that believeth not shall be damned." (Mormon 9:23)

Moroni concludes his writings in his father's record by saying "Behold I speak unto you as though I spake from the dead; for I know that ye shall have my words." (Moroni 9:30) He also tells us that the records are written in reformed Egyptian rather than Hebrew because of the limited space upon the plates. They would have been written in Hebrew if there had been more room to write, and in that case there would have been no imperfections in the record, but in reality there just simply wasn't enough space on the plates.

He warns people to not condemn the imperfections of the writings because of the errors or awkwardness in the writing mechanics. He indicates that the Lord will prepare a means of interpretation that will take care of any imperfections, all this in order to bring to pass the restoration of the knowledge of Christ to Moroni's brethren, the Lamanites, the covenant people and last remnant of the house of Israel in this land. (Mormon 9:)

*   *   *

REFORMED EGYPTIAN

Daniel C. Peterson: "The Book of Mormon claims to have been written in "reformed Egyptian" (Mormon 9:32). Most who have studied the subject conclude that this signifies writing the Hebrew language in modified Egyptian characters. In recent years, we have learned that several ancient documents were written in precisely that fashion." Daniel C. Peterson, "Mounting Evidence for the Book of Mormon," Ensign, Jan. 2000

*   *   *

THE BOOK OF ETHER

Moroni the 2nd edited and included the Book of Ether in his own records. The book of Ether and the history of the Jaredites have already been discussed at the beginning of this book in its proper chronological order. Most of it covers a time period long before the time of Lehi, but the records were not discovered until the time of Mosiah the Second in 121 B.C. by a failed expedition of the people of King Limhi who were looking for the city of Zarahemla. Later, the newly converted Nephite King Limhi turned the Jaredite records over to King Mosiah the 2nd for translation and safekeeping.

More than four hundred years after Christ's birth, Moroni the 2nd received the Jaredite records along with the other sacred records from his father, Mormon. Moroni then edited, abridged, and incorporated the Jaredite history into the Book of Mormon, as we know it today. Finally, fourteen hundred years later, Joseph Smith translated the records for us, in what we know as the book of Ether. It is not known whether Moroni used the Mosiah the Second translation as an aid in his own translation, or if it was all from his own hand and therefore a totally new translation from the original Jaredite plates of his own work.

This historical record of the Jaredites covers a period of time from the Tower of Babel in approximately 2000 B.C., all the way down to the time of the last surviving Jaredite, Coriantumr who lived with the Mulekites for nine months. This then points to a time reference that could not be before the people of Mulek left Jerusalem in 587 B.C. nor any later than 200 B.C. when Mosiah the 1st came to Zarahemla. Therefore this recorded history of the Jaredites must cover a time period of at least 1400 years, and possibly more than 2000 years. Unfortunately, the scriptural timeline for the Jaredite civilization is unclear.

Amaleki, who was the last record keeper on the small plates of Nephi, spoke of a large stone discovered in the days of King Mosiah the 1st. The stone was engraved with an account of the previously mentioned Jaredite king, Coriantumr.

"And they gave an account of one Coriantumr, and the slain of his people. And Coriantumr was discovered by the people of Zarahemla; and he dwelt with them for the space of nine moons." (Omni 1:21)

It was three generations later, during the time of King Mosiah the 2nd, that King Limhi turned the Jaredite history written on the Twenty Four Gold Plates over to King Mosiah the 2nd in Zarahemla. Some five hundred years later when these same records ended up in the hands of Moroni the 2nd, he wrote, "He that wrote this record was Ether, and he was a descendant of Coriantor." (Ether 1:6) Then Moroni proceeded with the complete genealogy of the prophet Ether from Coriantor all the way back to Jared who came with the Brother of Jared from the Tower of Babel to the Americas some 4,000 years ago. (Ether 1:7-32) The prophet Ether was the last of the Jaredite prophets and the last Jaredite record keeper.

Ether lived in the days of Coriantumr the 2nd, which was the last King of the Jaredites. After being driven to the necessity of hiding in a cave to protect himself from the unrepentant Jaredites, the Lord told the prophet Ether to go to King Coriantumr the 2nd and warn him as to what would happen if he and all of his household did not repent. Even though they heard the warning of a prophet, King Coriantumr and his household did not repent and so they did suffer the sad consequences of their grave sins eventually resulting in the total destruction of the Jaredite civilization.

Moroni says that he, himself, did not even write one hundredth of the record of Ether that was engraved up on the 24 gold plates. This was probably because it covered such a large time span, at least 1800 years or more of Jaredite history.

*   *   *

Encyclopedia of Mormonism, Vol.1, BOOK OF MORMON PEOPLES—ETHER

"The existing record is a summary by Moroni 2, last custodian of the Nephite records, of a history written on gold plates by Ether, the final Jaredite prophet, around the middle of the first Millennium B.C. Shaped by the editorial hands of Ether, Moroni 2, and Mosiah 2 (Mosiah 28:11-17), and by the demand for brevity, the account gives but a skeltal narrative covering more than two milliennia of Jaredite history. Most of it concerns just one of the eight lineages, Jared's, the ruling line to which Ether belonged, hence the name Jaredites."

*   *   *

Encyclopedia of Mormonism: "The final battle reported by Ether took place at the hill Ramah, the same place where Mormon later buried the sacred Nephite records (Ether 15:11). The war involved two vast armies, and hostilities continued several days until all the soldiers and one of the kings were slain. An exhausted Coriantumr culminated his victory over Shiz by decapitating him. Near Eastern examples of decapitation of enemies are evident in early art and literature, as on the Narmer palette; and decapitation of captured kings is represented in ancient Mesoamerica (Warren, pp. 230-33). Coriantumr was later discovered by the people of Zarahemla (Mulekites), with whom he lived for "nine moons" (Omni 1.21). Ether's plates (historical records), together with the decayed remains from the final Jaredite battle were later found by a group of lost Nephites who were searching for the city of Zarahemla." (Mosiah 8:8-11)—Encyclopedia of Mormonism, Vol.2, JAREDITES

*   *   *

Before leaving the book of Ether, certainly a mention of the Brother of Jared, the original "patriarch" of the Jaredites, would be an appropriate addendum and an inspiration to us all.

The faith of the Brother of Jared is legendary. As he was preparing the submarine-like barges for the journey across the great sea to the Americas, he asked the Lord to touch sixteen stones to provide light inside the eight barges during the long voyage. The Lord stretched out his hand and then with the veil removed, the Brother of Jared actually saw the finger of the Lord touching the stones. Being shocked that the Lord had a body "like unto flesh and blood"; he fell to the ground with fear. Then the Lord showed himself to the Brother of Jared saying,

"I am Jesus Christ . . . And never have I showed myself unto man whom I have created, for never has man believed in me as thou hast . . ." (Ether 3:14-15)

*   *   *

The brother of Jared was highly favored by the Lord and the Lord did minister to him where in he did have a "perfect knowledge of God". Yet even though he was commanded to treasure these things, he was also commanded to show them to no man. He was told to write of his special knowledge and testimony "in a language that cannot be read", and then seal it up along with the two stones, the Urim and Thummim, until a time when the Lord should choose that the records should be interpreted, and then and only then to be shown to the children of men. Lastly, he was given an unbelievable privilege. He was shown an astounding and miraculous vision of the past and the future of all the inhabitants of the earth.

Moroni the 2nd writes that he himself, was commanded by the Lord to write the things that the Bother of Jared saw, but that he should seal them up and hide them in the earth that they should not come forth until the day that the Gentiles do repent of their iniquities and are clean before the Lord. (Ether 4:6)

*   *   *

The Book of Mormon never mentions what the real name of the Brother of Jared happened to be. But in the process of blessing a child in the early days of the church, the prophet Joseph Smith gave the baby the name of Mahonri Moriancumer, explaining to the parents and others present, that it was the true name of The Brother of Jared and that it had just been revealed to him. See Bruce R. McConkie, Mormon Doctrine, p.463 MAHONRI MORIANCUMER

*   *   *

After recounting the extraordinary story of the Brother of Jared actually seeing the finger of God because of his great faith, Moroni then reveals that he, himself, had seen Jesus face to face. "And then shall ye know that I have seen Jesus, and that he hath talked with me face to face . . ." (Ether 12:39)

As Moroni the 2nd continued writing what we now know as the Book of Moroni, he reveals that after abridging the records of the people of Jared in the book of Ether, he really had no intention of writing any more upon the plates or continuing to make more records because he was forced into running and hiding from the Lamanites.

The Lamanites were not only killing every last Nephite who refused to deny Christ, but they were warring among themselves with great violence. Moroni said that he could not and would not deny Christ; therefore he hid from the Lamanites, but was inspired to write a few more words so that these words might be of worth to his Lamanite brethren in the future.

In Moroni chapters two through seven, we are given a virtual tutorial on many important religious precepts and gospel principals. Moroni outlines the basics of the ordinances and blessings, including the laying on of hands for the gift of the Holy Ghost, the ordaining of priest and teachers, and in addition, the exact wording of the blessings to be pronounced upon the bread and wine of the sacred Sacrament. He continues with such gospel principles as a broken heart and contrite spirit, true repentance and baptism, fasting and prayer, and conducting by the power of the Holy Ghost. He mentions praying with real intent, and the giving to others without doing it grudgingly; otherwise it will not be counted to you for good. He continues, "A bitter fountain can not bring forth good water . . ." "The spirit of Christ is given to every man, that he may know good from evil . . ." He emphasizes that if miracles and the administering of angels seems to have ceased, it is because of the lack of faith. He stresses that if we don't possess charity, we have nothing, for it is the "pure love of Christ."

Obviously, reading the full account of Moroni's writings in the Book of Moroni would be a very valuable study to anyone interested in having a spiritual guide, an inspired reference to show us the way that we can obtain true happiness through the way we conduct our lives. One might say that Moroni's writings are like a valuable "How to Book" on how to serve Christ and our fellowmen, as well as an aid to finding happiness.

In chapter eight, Moroni recounts the writing of his father Mormon in a letter specifically written to Moroni. After praising his son for his faithfulness, his father Mormon mentions something that does grieve him "exceedingly", namely the baptism of small children before they are accountable. Mormon calls the baptizing of children, a perversion of the ways of the Lord, which denies the mercies of Christ, and people who do it, are in danger of death and the torments of Hell. As Mormon ends his letter to his son, he declares that because of the pride of the Nephite people and their refusal to repent, and their denial of God's authority, and the denying of the Holy Ghost, the Nephite people, unfortunately, will soon perish in fulfillment of prophecy. (Moroni 8:)

In Moroni chapter nine, there is another letter from Mormon to his son Moroni. In this letter, he reveals that many of the choicest leaders in his army have been killed, and the people flatly refuse to listen to his warnings and admonishments and he writes that they even "anger against me." The spirit of the Lord totally ceased to strive with Mormon's people, as they thirsted after blood and revenge continually. Mormon asks a timely and relevant question that pertains to his time and to our own time. "How can we expect that God will stay his hand in judgment against us?" (Moroni 9:14)

*   *   *

KINGDOMS OF THIS WORLD
—GOVERNMENTS OF MEN

"In brief, such is the story told in the Book of Mormon of the ancient inhabitants of America . . . They worshiped the true and living God, in a land which is dedicated to his worship and held in reserve for a righteous people, until they became confirmed transgressors. Let the Gentiles upon this land heed the warning and serve Jesus Christ, lest destruction also come upon them, for it has been prophesied that the present inhabitants if they turn from the worship of the true and living God shall bring down upon them the same destruction, "as the inhabitants of the land have hitherto done." Doctrines of Salvation, Volume 3—Chapter 16

*   *   *

Quote from PRESIDENT ABRAHAM LINCOLN

[President] "Lincoln said that if we as a people do not turn to God and serve him, our nation will drift into destruction. He expressed his meaning in these words: 'If we do not do right, God will let us go our own way to ruin. If we do right, he will lead us safely out of this wilderness and crown our arms with victory.' Thereupon he summoned America to turn to God as the only means of survival." Mark E. Petersen, Conference Report, April 1968, p.60

*   *   *

President Lincoln gave that inspired warning back in the dark days of the Civil war, more than 140 years ago. We find it to be very similar to the same warnings that the Book of Mormon prophets have proclaimed many times, spanning a thousand years of time all the way from Nephi in 600 B.C. to Moroni in 400 A.D. Our modern day prophets have given us these same warnings; which is to either turn to God and obey his commandments or suffer the consequences. Will the people of the America fail to listen to these grave warnings just as the Nephites did? Will our own society pay heed to these vital lessons from history or will they ignore them resulting in a great suffering of this people and the irreversible consequences, including the loss of our precious freedom?

Mormon then continues his letter to his son Moroni recounting the repulsive acts of the uncivilized behavior of the people, and the unbelievable atrocities committed by both the Lamanites and the Nephites in their great hatred towards each other.

"And they have become strong in their perversion; and they are alike brutal, sparing none, neither old nor young; and they delight in everything save that which is good; and the suffering of our women and our children upon all the face of this land doth exceed everything; yea tongue cannot tell, neither can it be written." (Moroni 9:19)

Starving the Nephite women and children which they had imprisoned, the Lamanites then fed them the flesh of their own murdered fathers and husbands. Not to be outdone, the Nephite warriors took the captured Lamanite women, raped them, tortured them to death, and then ate their flesh as a "token of bravery."

These atrocities seem to be beyond just evil, and the depravity of both sides is beyond belief. The spirit of the Lord was completely gone and Satan reigned strong upon the land and the people totally refused to listen to Mormon, as he declared that the wickedness of the Nephites goes beyond even the Lamanites, which would most certainly lead to their own extinction.

As noted in the previous chapter, the few Nephites who would survive the destruction would be intermingled with the Lamanites and numbered with them, fulfilling the promise to Joseph who was sold into Egypt that "thy seed shall not utterly be destroyed." (see Alma 45:14 and 1st Nephi 13:30) Both these scriptures infer that although the Nephites as a people would be completely destroyed, every last one of the Nephites as individuals would not be destroyed in totality.

On a more positive note, as Mormon bade farewell to his son, he encouraged him to be faithful in Christ, not to be unduly grieved by what he had told him, and to be lifted up by the grace of God and his son Jesus Christ who sits on the right hand of God. (Moroni 9:)

The last chapter of Moroni and the final chapter of the Book of Mormon contains the great and powerful words that have caused millions of people around the world to gain a testimony of the Book of Mormon.

"And when ye shall receive these things, I would exhort you that ye would ask God, the Eternal Father, in the name of Jesus Christ, if these things are not true, and if ye shall ask with sincere heart, with real intent, having faith in Christ, he will manifest the truth of it unto you by the power of the Holy Ghost." (Moroni 10:4) If you haven't been clued in yet, this verse is an extraordinarily and marvelous promise to those who sincerely read the Book of Mormon.

Moroni then makes a soul piercing and powerful statement; that we should remember these things because the time "doth speedingly" come when we shall see him at the bar of God, and God will ask; "Did I not declare my words unto you, which were written by this man, like one crying from the dead, yea, even as one speaking from the dust." (Moroni 10:27)

Moroni concludes by urging all to come unto Christ, being perfected in him, and to deny all ungodliness, and to love God with all our might, mind, and strength. Then he bids us farewell saying that he soon goes to rest in the paradise of God and that he will meet us before the pleasing bar of the Great Jehovah. Amen (Moroni 10:)

*   *   *

THE ANGEL MORONI

After Moroni the 2nd passed from this mortal life, he became a resurrected messenger of God and a most important figure in restoring the true Church of Jesus Christ upon the face of the Earth once again. He was the heavenly being that was instrumental in divinely bringing forth the Book of Mormon for the benefit of the House of Israel and the World. No wonder we find his likeness in a golden figure topping our temples worldwide.

*   *   *

Encyclopedia of Mormonism, Vol.2, MORONI, ANGEL

"The angel Moroni is the heavenly messenger who first visited the Prophet Joseph Smith in 1823. As a mortal named Moroni 2, he had completed the compilation and writing of the Book of Mormon. He ministered to Joseph Smith as a resurrected being, in keeping with his responsibility for the Book of Mormon, inasmuch as "the keys of the record of the stick of Ephraim" had been committed to him by the Lord (D&C 27:5). Pursuant to this responsibility he first appeared to Joseph Smith on the night of September 21-22, 1823 (JS—H 1:29-49; D&C 128:20), and thereafter counseled with him in several reappearances until the book was published in 1830. During that time, he instructed Joseph Smith, testified to the Three Witnesses of the Book of Mormon, and otherwise assisted in the work of restoring the gospel."

*   *   *

The Angel Moroni didn't just drop the Gold plates in the boy Joseph's lap and leave the naïve boy guessing as what to do next. He instructed and taught Joseph from his first appearance to the boy at age seventeen in 1823, until the time that Joseph was finally allowed to take the plates from their resting place in the Hill Cumorah in 1827, at age twenty-one.

*   *   *

"The messenger did not limit his instruction solely to these annual meetings, but made contact with Joseph on numerous occasions (Peterson, pp. 119-20). In all, the angel Moroni visited Joseph Smith at least twenty times." (see Moroni, Visitations of). Encyclopedia of Mormonism, Vol.4, VISIONS OF JOSEPH SMITH

*   *   *

The Angel Moroni was a major instrument in bringing about the restoration of the Gospel of Jesus Christ as he delivered the precious words contained in the sacred scriptures that we now call the Book of Mormon. Nephi wrote; "Angels speak by the power of the Holy Ghost; wherefore, they speak the words of Christ. Wherefore, I said unto you, feast upon the words of Christ; for behold, the words of Christ will tell you all things what ye should do." (2 Nephi 32:3)

Maybe, but just maybe, the words that the Angel Moroni brought to us through the Book of Mormon really are the "words of Christ" and the book that he brought Joseph Smith would actually help us to feast upon the words of Christ "telling us all things what we should do" in order to live a happier life. Moroni was one of the major agents in restoring the Gospel of Jesus Christ back to the earth. In the New Testament, John the Revelator describes some of the things that will come to past in the last days when the Lamb returns. As latter Day Saints, we believe that John foretold of the Angel Moroni's ministry in those last days.

"And I saw another angel fly in the midst of heaven, having the everlasting gospel to preach unto them that dwell on the earth, and to every nation, and kindred, and tongue and people." (Revelations 14:6)

Fulfilling the words of John the Revelator's vision, the Angel Moroni did bring forth the Book of Mormon in the last days, and in a divine manner did deliver it to Joseph Smith Jr. at the Hill Cumorah. The Prophet then translated it under the inspiration of the Lord and saw to it that it would be published for all that desired to read it. Since that time, the sacred words and the "everlasting gospel" which it contains has been printed in dozens of languages, and has been taken by a great army of LDS missionaries around the world to many tongues, kindred, and nations. Thus, it has been now introduced to many people in many lands, and for those who are sincere in heart and ready and willing to hear the words of Christ and act upon them, it has given them a new and brighter life far beyond their own expectations, even beyond their own hoped for dreams of a more worthwhile life and a greater happiness.

*   *   *

CHAPTER TWENTY

* * *

A MOST REMARKABLE BOOK OF ANCIENT ORIGIN

There is no question that the Book of Mormon is a most unusual and a very remarkable book, and there are more than a few interesting facts and fascinating bits of information about it that arouse curiosity, great interest, and substantiate its many evidences of authenticity. There are some especially thought provoking aspects pertaining to its very existence that are intriguing, perhaps a little mysterious, and in so many ways miraculous and inspirational.

First on the list of interesting facts is the Title Page? Who wrote it? What is its significance and why is it important? The Encyclopedia of Mormonism states:

"According to the title page, the Book of Mormon is addressed to Lamanites, Jews, and gentiles and is designed to inform Lamanites of promises made to their forebears and to convince 'Jew and Gentile that Jesus is the Christ, the Eternal God, manifesting himself unto all nations.'

Joseph Smith once wrote, 'I wish to mention here that the title-page of the Book of Mormon is a literal translation, taken from the very last leaf, on the left hand side of the collection or book of plates, which contained the record which has been translated; . . . and that said title-page is not . . . a modern composition, either of mine or of any other man who has lived or does live in this generation.'" (HC 1:71.). Encyclopedia of Mormonism, Vol.1, BOOK OF MORMON

*   *   *

There is an ancient practice in Middle East writing called "scriptorio", which places the title page at the END of a book, instead of at the beginning. This is something that is a trademark of ancient writings from that area, and is another strong evidence of the authenticity of the Book of Mormon. It is highly unlikely that Joseph Smith or any of his associates had even heard of this practice when he translated the gold plates, but he makes the comment that the title page was "taken from the very last leaf, on the left hand side of the collection or book of plates." see www.jefflindsay.com/BMEvidences.shtml

So then, this being uncharacteristic of normal authoring and publishing procedures and unfamiliar to Joseph Smith, he found that the title page was on the last page of the records instead of at the beginning of the book as was the common practice in the printing of books in his day and in ours. This would be a very unusual and unlikely thing for an uneducated farm boy to think up and to incorporate into his book if he was fabricating it on his own. The title page also reminds all of the Book of Mormon critics, as well as all of the rest of us, that . . .

"If there are faults they are the mistakes of men; wherefore, condemn not the things of God."

* * *

THE MYSTERY OF THE METAL PLATES

The sacred records are often referred to as plates, for the obvious reason that they were actually engraved upon metal plates, very thin sheets of metal such as brass or gold. Many critics have made fun of Joe Smith's bible written on gold metal plates and his mention of a Hebrew Bible written on brass plates. However, archeologists have now found abundant examples of ancient writings on metal plates of brass, copper, tin and even gold.

A very important example of writing on metal plates, which is thousands of years old, was found by non-LDS archeologists in recent times. It was engraved in eighteenth century B.C. on "copper plates" and was found to be ancient Byblos Syllabic inscriptions from the ancient Phoenician coastal city of Byblos. The script itself is described as, "syllabary [which] is clearly inspired by the Egyptian hieroglyphic system, and in fact is the most important link known between the hieroglyphs and the Canaanite alphabet."

Although many skeptics laughed at Joseph Smith and his book written on metal plates, recent archeological discoveries have shown that writing on metal plates was not only well established as an ancient practice, but was a particularly significant practice in the Middle East around the time when Father Lehi lived in 600 B.C., and was especially used for religious purposes. *See Article in July 1994 F.A.R.M.S. Update, Number 95, by the Foundation for Ancient Research and Mormon Studies*

*   *   *

The sacred words and history contained on the gold plates that the Prophet Joseph Smith received at Hill Cumorah, came from a number of unique original sources; those sources having come from compiled abridgments, epistles, narratives, and quotes derived from and originally written upon several different sets of ancient metal plates by several different authors. The following is a list of the plate sources from which the writings of the Book of Mormon were derived from: (1) the plates of brass; (2) the records of Lehi; (3) the large plates of Nephi; (4) the small plates of Nephi; (5) the plates of Mormon; and (6) the twenty-four gold plates of Ether. Encyclopedia of Mormonism, Vol.1, BOOK OF MORMON PLATES AND RECORDS

*   *   *

When the ancient prophet called Mormon put the Book of Mormon all together, he placed along with the small plates of Nephi his own abridgment of the large plates of Nephi, which he had written in his own words, as well as inserting occasional editorial comments. Sometimes he would include a first person account such as he did from Zeniff's narrative when his people left Zarahemla. Many sermons, blessings, and epistles are quoted directly from their original sources. Such was the case with many of the chapters from the Old Testament prophet Isaiah, as well as Zenos and Zenoch, which were quoted directly from the Plates of Brass, this giving an indication of their importance. See 1 Nephi chapter 19

Finally, Mormon's son Moroni, completed the plates of Mormon, abridged the plates of Ether, and added his own observations and thoughts, and then buried this combined set of sacred records for safe keeping until the time appointed by the Lord, when they would come forth from out of the dust. As members of the church, we believe that the prophet Isaiah spoke of the Book of Mormon itself, in some detail thousands of years ago:

*　　*　　*

Isaiah 29:4 And thou shalt be brought down, [and] shalt speak out of the ground, and thy speech shall be low out of the dust, and thy voice shall be, as of one that hath a familiar spirit, out of the ground, and thy speech shall whisper out of the dust.

Isaiah 29:11 And the vision of all is become unto you as the words of a book that is sealed, which [men] deliver to one that is learned, saying, Read this, I pray thee: and he saith, I cannot; for it [is] sealed:

Isaiah 29:12 And the book is delivered to him that is not learned, saying, Read this, I pray thee: and he saith, I am not learned.

*　　*　　*

The respected LDS author and apostle, James E. Talmage comments on Isaiah's words in his book, "Articles of Faith."

"Isaiah's striking prediction that the nation thus brought down should "speak out of the ground," with speech "low out of the dust" was literally fulfilled in the bringing forth of the Book of Mormon, the original of which was taken out of the ground, and the voice of the record is as that of one speaking from the dust. In continuation of the same prophecy we read: "And the vision of all is become unto you as the words of a book that is sealed, which men deliver to one that is learned, saying, Read this, I pray thee: and he saith, I cannot; for it is sealed: And the book is delivered to him that is not learned, saying, Read this, I pray thee: and he saith, I am not learned." The fulfilment of this prediction is claimed in the presentation of the transcript from the plates—"the words of a book," not the book itself—to the learned Professor Charles Anthon, whose reply, almost in the words of the text, has been cited in the last chapter; and in the delivery of the book itself to the unlettered youth, Joseph Smith."—James E. Talmage, Articles of Faith, Ch.14, p.269

*   *   *

Joseph Smith himself wrote the following description of the plates in his famous Wentworth letter, a letter that the Prophet wrote to John Wentworth, the editor of a Chicago newspaper, in response to his inquiry about Mormonism.

"These records were engraven on plates which had the appearance of gold, each plate was six inches wide and eight inches long, and not quite so thick as common tin. They were filled with engravings, in Egyptian characters, and bound together in a volume as the leaves of a book, with three rings running through the whole. The volume was something near six inches in thickness, a part of which was sealed. The characters on the unsealed part were small, and beautifully engraved. The whole book exhibited many marks of antiquity in its construction, and much skill in the art of engraving. With the records was found a curious instrument, which the ancients called "Urim and Thummim," which consisted of two transparent stones set in the rim of a bow fastened to a breastplate. Through the medium of the Urim and Thummim I translated the record by the gift and power of God." History of the Church, Vol.4, Ch.31, p.537

*   *   *

The highly respected General Authority, Apostle and LDS author, Bruce R, McConkie helps us gain a clearer picture of exactly what was on the Gold plates.

Bruce R. McConkie, Mormon Doctrine, p.326 GOLD PLATES

"As we now have it, the Book of Mormon is a translation of a portion of the Gold Plates. These plates came into being in the following way: Nephi made two sets of plates which are known as the Large Plates of Nephi and the Small Plates of Nephi. Upon the Large Plates he abridged the records of his father, Lehi, and began a detailed history of his people, including their wars, contentions, the reign of their kings, and their genealogy. The Small Plates he reserved for sacred writings, prophecies, and things pertaining to the ministry. (1 Ne. 1:17; 9; 19:1-6; 2 Ne. 4:14; 5:30, 33; Jac. 1:1-4.) These plates were handed down from prophet to prophet, and by about 130 B.C., some [470] years after Lehi left Jerusalem, the Small Plates were full. (Omni 1:30)

Mormon made the Plates of Mormon on which he abridged the Large Plates of Nephi and to which he added without abridgment the Small Plates of Nephi. (Words of Morm. 1-11.) Both Mormon and Moroni wrote some things of their own on the Plates of Mormon, and Moroni also wrote on them an abridgment of Jaredite history taken from the Plates of Ether. Thus when the Gold Plates were placed in the Hill Cumorah, they contained a record of both the Nephites and the Jaredites." Bruce R. McConkie, Mormon Doctrine, p.454 LOST SCRIPTURE

Journal of Discourses: "We have only a minor part of the scriptures had by the Jaredites. (Ether 1:1-5; 4:1-7.) There were many records in the hands of Mormon when he compiled, abridged, and wrote the Book of Mormon, none of which records are known to us now. (Words of Morm. 1-11.) It is reported by President Brigham Young that there was in the Hill Cumorah a room containing many wagon loads of plates." (Journal of Discourses, vol. 19, p. 38.)

*   *   *

As wonderful and enlightening as the Book of Mormon is, and even though it appears to be very complete with more than 500 pages of history, vast wisdom, and great spiritual knowledge, we never-the-less are told that we only have a portion of what was actually on the Gold Plates. Joseph Fielding Smith Jr. wrote the following concerning that idea.

REVELATIONS WITHHELD BECAUSE OF UNBELIEF.

"Now the Lord is withholding from us a great many truths that he would gladly reveal if we were ready to receive them. Did you know that a portion of the record from which the Book of Mormon is taken is sealed? The Prophet was not permitted to break the seals, and we will not receive the sealed record until the time comes when the people will show by their faith their willingness to accept it." Joseph Fielding Smith Jr., Doctrines of Salvation, Vol.3, p.201-p.202

*   *   *

So why is it that we don't we have the rest of the book of Mormon, the sealed part? Wouldn't there be important gospel principles, worthy admonitions, and great religious truths in the sealed part of it too, all of which would be of great value to us as members of the church? President Kimball offered this almost humorous insight on the subject.

Spencer W. Kimball, "I have had many people ask me through the years, "When do you think we will get the balance of the Book of Mormon records?" And I have said, "How many in the congregation would like to read the sealed portion of the plates?" And almost always there is a 100-percent response. And then I ask the same congregation, "How many of you have read the part that has been opened to us?" And there are many who have not read the Book of Mormon, the unsealed portion. We are quite often looking for the spectacular, the unobtainable. I have found many people who want to live the higher laws when they do not live the lower laws." The Teachings of Spencer W. Kimball, p.531

*   *   *

THE HILL CUMORAH

The hill in New York, which we as members of the church call Cumorah, is a highly celebrated and most important place in church history, the "birth place" of the Book of Mormon. Yet there are some unanswered questions about it, which arouse great curiosity among many members of the church. Is the hill Cumorah in New York the exact same hill that was called Cumorah by the Nephites and the same hill called "Ramah" by the Jaredites? Is the hill where the prophet Mormon buried the sacred records during the last great battle and final destruction of the Nephite people, the exact same hill where Joseph Smith unearthed and received the sacred records from the angel Moroni in the state of New York? Do we really know for sure? Let me point out some interesting facts that leave this very question piquing at our curiosity, while at the same time, we can expand our understanding, knowledge, and general impressions of the Hill Cumorah, even if we might not obtain fully satisfying answers to the above questions.

*   *   *

The GLOSSARY in the appendix of the Encyclopedia of Mormonism defines Cumorah in the following way . . . Encyclopedia of Mormonism, Vol.4, Appendix 2

"Cumorah*

(1) A hill in which the Book of Mormon prophet Mormon concealed sacred records before the annihilation of his people;

(2) The hill in New York State, near the town of Palmyra, where Joseph Smith unearthed the gold plates from which he translated the Book of Mormon."

*   *   *

Notice that there are two separate and completely different entries in the glossary for Cumorah, leaving the question wide open as to whether they are the same hill. Although the great majority of the members of the church assume that the Hill Cumorah in New York is one in the same as the Hill Cumorah described in the Book of Mormon, Joseph Smith never unequivocally designated the hill from which he took the gold plates as being Cumorah, nor did he call it by that specific name. He only uses the name Cumorah once in his writings and that was twelve years after the Book of Mormon was published, wherein he used the name Cumorah in D&C 128:20. "And again, what do we hear? Glad tidings from Cumorah!" Just which Cumorah is he referring to as the source of these "Glad Tidings" in this statement; the one in New York or the one in the Book of Mormon? In his own writings, he only makes reference to an unnamed hill from which he took the plates. In his own history, he describes in some detail the resting place of the plates without naming the hill specifically.

Joseph Smith History 1:51 "Convenient to the village of Manchester, Ontario county, New York, stands a hill of considerable size, and the most elevated of any in the neighborhood. On the west side of this hill, not far from the top, under a stone of considerable size, lay the plates, deposited in a stone box."

Later in his writings, he again refers to it as a hill in Manchester, but once again without specifically naming it.

"Moroni, who deposited the plates in a hill in Manchester, Ontario County, New York, being dead and raised again there from, appeared unto me, and told me where they were, and gave me directions how to obtain them. I obtained them, and the Urim and Thummim with them, by the means of which I translated the plates; and thus came the Book of Mormon."

Teachings of the Prophet Joseph Smith, Section Three 1838-39 p.119

The hill "convenient to the village of Manchester" did not receive its name, Cumorah, until after the Book of Mormon was published, at which time many of Joseph's associates began calling it by that name. We do not know if they just assumed that it was the same hill spoken of in the Book of Mormon where Mormon buried the plates, or if Joseph had actually indicated that it was the same hill. At any length, he did not correct his associates when they called "the hill" in New York, Cumorah. Perhaps, Joseph thought that it was as good of name as any, and it certainly did seem appropriate.

* * *

Joseph Fielding Smith Jr., Doctrines of Salvation, Vol.3, p.234
"Further, the fact that all of his associates from the beginning down have spoken of it as the identical hill where Mormon and Moroni hid the records, must carry some weight. It is difficult for a reasonable person to believe that such men as Oliver Cowdery. Brigham Young, Parley P. Pratt, Orson Pratt, David Whitmer, and many others, could speak frequently of the Spot where the Prophet Joseph Smith obtained the plates as the Hill Cumorah, and not be corrected by the Prophet, if that were not the fact. That they did speak of this hill in the days of the Prophet in this definite manner is an established record of history."

"While in this statement it is not positively declared that the Hill Cumorah is the place where the plates were obtained, yet the implication that such is the case is overwhelming." Joseph Fielding Smith Jr., Doctrines of Salvation, Vol.3, p.237

* * *

Encyclopedia of Mormonism, Vol.1, CUMORAH
"Cumorah in the Book of Mormon refers to a hill and surrounding area where the final battle between the Nephites and Lamanites took place, resulting in the annihilation of the Nephite people (see Book of Mormon Peoples). Sensing the impending destruction of his people, Mormon records that he concealed the plates of Nephi 1

and all the other records entrusted to him in a hill called Cumorah to prevent them from falling into the hands of the Lamanites (see Book of Mormon Plates and Records). He delivered his own abridgment of these records, called the plates of Mormon, and the small plates of Nephi, which he placed with them, to his son Moroni 2, **who continued writing on them before burying them in an unmentioned site more than thirty-six years later."** (W of M 1:5; Morm. 6:6) (Moroni 10:1-2). (The underlining and emphasis added by this author)

According to the scriptures, Mormon turned the plates over to Moroni in 385 A.D., but Moroni, in his own words said that he did not seal up the records until 420 years after the signs of Christ's Birth, some thirty-six years later. So where and how far did he wander during those thirty-six years? In all reality, we are not certain where the unmentioned burial site is located. Therefore we are not sure in just exactly what hill Moroni did finally end up burying the Gold Plates. Without naming any specific place or saying where it was, he writes only "And I seal up these records." Furthermore, we are certainly not sure how the plates got to a hill in New York, whether that be by the physical efforts and the limited human strength of Moroni as a mortal man, or were they moved about by the divine kinetics of Moroni's heavenly powers as an angel and as a sacred messenger of God?

Since it is more than 3000 miles from the plausible "narrow neck of land" Book of Mormon locations in Mesoamerica to the far away state of New York in the eastern United States, and given that those plates were made of gold and were extremely heavy and awkward, the latter seems the most likely scenario; that is that the plates were moved "hither and thither" by Moroni's divine powers.

*   *   *

Encyclopedia of Mormonism, Vol.1

"In 1928 the Church purchased the western New York hill and in 1935 erected a monument recognizing the visit of the angel Moroni. Each summer since 1937, the Church has staged the Cumorah Pageant at this site. Entitled America's Witness for Christ, it depicts important events from Book of Mormon history. This annual pageant has reinforced the common assumption that Moroni buried the plates of Mormon in the same hill where his father had buried the other plates, thus equating this New York hill with the Book of Mormon Cumorah. Because the New York site does not readily fit the Book of Mormon description of Book of Mormon geography, some Latter-day Saints have looked for other possible explanations and locations, including Mesoamerica. Although some have identified possible sites that may seem to fit better, there are no conclusive connections between the Book of Mormon text and any specific site that has been suggested."—Encyclopedia of Mormonism, Vol.1, CUMORAH

*   *   *

Now, keeping in mind that within the pages of the Book of Mormon that there are two cities called Jerusalem, and also that there are two different places called Bountiful, isn't it possible that there could also be two different Hill Cumorahs? If after reading all this, you are thoroughly confused and still left somewhat unsatisfied in trying to decide if there were two different Hill Cumorahs or just one, then you are certainly not alone. The Cumorah question cannot be answered definitively at this point in time.

However, in the final analysis, it does not matter whether the hill at Palmyra New York was the exact same hill where the prophet Mormon originally buried the sacred records, or if it is actually a second hill named after the original hill Cumorah, which may have been in reality located in an area north of the narrow neck of land in Mesoamerica (that is Guatemala-Mexico).

The thing of ultimate importance is that the Lord through the Angel Moroni, divinely placed the sacred records in the hands of Joseph Smith Jr. in New York state to be translated for the benefit of the descendants of a remnant of the House of Israel and to the Gentiles, and most importantly to be ANOTHER TESTAMENT TO THE DIVINITY OF JESUS CHRIST to the entire world.

*   *   *

COULD JOSEPH SMITH HAVE FABRICATED THE BOOK OF MORMON?

Many skeptical and uninformed people in past history and even around the world today, still believe that the Book of Mormon is a concoction of Joseph Smith's imagination. Only after careful reading and studying the book, can one see the full absurdity of an "untravelled" farm boy, with a grammar school education, writing such a significant religious volume. Here is a book that is filled with numerous unique traits of the ancient Middle East culture, Semitic language patterns and root words, and even Hebrew poetic forms and idioms, which a young farm boy in nineteenth century New York couldn't possibly have known.

It also bears mentioning, that this farm boy with a rudimentary education, and being a first time author, supposedly created and wrote this significant religious volume of more than 500 pages in a period of only sixty working days. This would be a monumental feat, even without being distracted by the taking care of his wife, and having to travel from town to town and state to state to escape harassment from his enemies. Most people in the church today have a difficult time just trying to read the Book of Mormon in sixty days, even as they sit in the safety and comfort of their easy chair.

Even if one has not gained a testimony of the divine origins of the Book of Mormon, no intelligent person can believe that Joseph Smith wrote or fabricated this book, given his background and education. Furthermore, even a highly educated professor of the 1830's could not have known or written of the many things that are detailed in the Book of Mormon which were simply not within the knowledge confines of western civilization in the nineteenth century. These things include such items as the knowledge of ancient cement buildings in Central America, many archaeological examples of ancient writings on metal plates from the Middle East, and the recent discovery of Papyrus Amherst # 63, which is a "Reformed Egyptian" like writing on a papyrus scroll that contains Aramaic texts written in demotic Egyptian script, very similar to the writings on the gold plates translated by Joseph Smith.

If Joseph Smith had made up the Book of Mormon, his imagination was uncannily accurate in the way that he described the travels of Lehi's family, in the detail of their compass directions, plausible routes used anciently, rare place names, and the perfect description of an unknown fertile valley at the edge of the Arabian sea, unknown in his time, but verified with technological navigation many decades later. Satellite imagery has facilitated the modern discovery of a lush secluded "Bountiful" like area along the endless barren desert coasts of the Arabian Peninsula that fits the description in the Book of Mormon. None of these things were known in Joseph Smith's time, even by the professors of great universities. The only logical explanation is that somebody who had actually traveled that route a couple of thousand years before Joseph Smith was even born, wrote about the arduous trip, left the record of their travels for posterity, and then by divine intervention, the record was recovered and delivered to the hands of Joseph Smith who translated it under divine influence.

In the book called "THE TRIAL OF THE STICK OF JOSEPH", law student and author Jack H. West reports that of the approximately 300 proper names found in the Book of Mormon, 180 of them were never heard of in western civilization before the Book of Mormon was published. It was discovered later that Central and South American Indian tribes that were not even known in 1830, had been using some of these 180 names for as long as they could remember. When an interviewer asked an Indian, "How long have you called that river over there Nephihah?"

The Indian replied, "As long as we can remember-always Nephihah-from chief to chief, from father to son, passed down-always Nephihah."

Similar stories were related regarding most of the other 180 names. (Jack H. West—"The Trial of the Stick of Joseph" c1981 p. 54-55)

Modern archeologist have found nine of these particular names used by the Bolivian Indians in their Aymara language and two more found in the Quicha language of the Peruvian Indians.

The strange name of "sheum" found in Mosiah 9:9, which was used there in a list of seeds and grains, was found by linguists to be an Akkadian cereal name dating back to the third millennium B.C. This was not known until at least 1857, twenty-seven years after the Book of Mormon was published. (see www.jefflindsay/ BMevidences.shtml)

In the Book of Mormon, the Nephites gave a place called "the land of Jershon" to the newly converted and reformed Lamanites as a place that they could live in peace while the Nephite armies protected them. Linguists have linked the name Jershon to a Hebrew root word meaning "to inherit" which is consistent with Alma 27:22 where the people of Anti-Nephi-Lehi were given the land of Jershon as "an inheritance." (www.jefflindsay/BMevidences.shtml)

Another unusual place name in the Book of Mormon, found in 1 Nephi 16:34 identifies the burial place where Nephi's father-in-law had died as Nahom. Modern archeologists have discovered an ancient site south east of Jerusalem on the Frankincense Trail that has traditionally been a place for burial and mourning. The rare place name Nehem/Nahom (nhm) is only found in one place on the Arabian Peninsula, and it is a place consistent with Nephi's description of their travels after leaving Jerusalem. Joseph Smith had no way of knowing about this rare place name during his day, which was only discovered in recent times by LDS scholars. Linguists have found that the Semitic use of the word Nahom is not only used to denote mourning or consolation, but also to infer groaning and complaining. This fits in perfectly with the Book of Mormon account of the daughters of Ishmael's great grief over their father's death, and is also reconcilable with their groaning and complaining against Father Lehi. They thought he had brought them all into the wilderness to starve and die.

(for further reading see www.jefflindsay/BMevidences.shtml)

There are a number of specific Middle Eastern idiosyncrasies, traits, and cultural mannerisms offhandedly mentioned in the Book of Mormon, which were almost certainly unknown to Joseph Smith;

such as the complete trust in a sacred oath even by an enemy, the "casting of lots" in decision making, "an alter of stone", "a river of water", and "plates of brass" rather than using the simple English of a stone alter, the brass plates, or just a river. Joseph Smith knew nothing about growing olives, nor did anyone that he knew; yet Jacob 5: goes on for several pages with the very pertinent details of growing olives in the ancient Middle East.

During the nineteenth century, it was believed by many uninformed people that Joseph Smith had copied the Book of Mormon from the work of Samuel Spaulding, a Pennsylvanian clergyman. In 1885, after a careful examination and comparison with the "Spaulding Manuscript", President James H. Fairchild of Oberlin College in Ohio, along with a colleague, declared that the Book of Mormon had no resemblance whatsoever to the Spaulding work, not a single sentence.

Joseph Smith was also accused of plagiarizing from Alexander von Humboldt, another contemporary author, geographer and world traveler, who wrote about South American and Mesoamerican geology, biology, and geography. Once again, even though some obscure parallels with the Book of Mormon have been made in very vague generalities, not a single detail, passage, or story line can be identified as having come from Humboldt's work, not to mention, that the subject matter and general themes of these two books have no similarity, whatsoever, with the Book of Mormon. (See www. jefflindsay/BMevidences.shtml)

Neither of the above secular works comes even close to resembling the historical content or the spiritual and religious nature of the Book of Mormon, nor does any other writings written by contemporary authors of Joseph Smith's time. Anti-Book of Mormon critics have yet to find any evidence what so ever of plagiarism by the Prophet.

*   *   *

Recent anti-Book of Mormon critics have said that DNA studies taken from the Native Americans in the far North of North America, demonstrates that these people have an Asian heritage and definitely not a Semitic heritage from the Middle East; therefore this proves that the Book of Mormon is fraudulent. They forgot to mention that the data samples were much too limited to be of any real sound scientific value. To be of any real value they should of collected the DNA from the many different Native American groups that are scattered all over the Western Hemisphere, including Mesoamerica, not just Eskimos.

Any true anthropologist can tell you that "Native Americans" as an ethnic group are definitely not a homogeneous people, but many highly diverse groups with different bloodlines, language roots, and many cultures varying widely from the primitive Inuit "Mongolian like" nomadic people of the far North to the highly cultured and civilized peoples of Central and South America who had a knowledge of mathematics, written languages, cement making, and advanced astronomy.

Certainly one can believe that there must have been Native American ancestors who most assuredly came across the Bering Strait from Asia during the ice age, but there is also undeniable evidence in North, Central, and South America of cultures far more akin to the "Egyptian like" Middle Eastern cultural influences than to the nomadic Asian cultures. So how did these supposed North country nomads, in such a short time, evolve into advanced cultures that were able to build well-organized cities, great temple pyramids, superior cement constructions, and use advanced astronomy and mathematics, and create the "Egyptian like" art styles and languages left in solid stone? Can those Bering Strait anthropologists legitimately continue to insist this is the only possibility for all Native American heritages?

In the book "America B.C." by Barry Fell 1976, the author has a photograph of Native American artwork picturing a catfish, but that catfish has the Libyo-Egyptian word N-A-R written on it, which means catfish in the Libyan Middle East. Among other interesting photos, he has a Libyan clay tablet found at Cuenca, Ecuador inscribed with Libyan lettering and an unmistakable image of an elephant, dating to possibly the latter half of third century B.C. The ancient Libyan sailors were extremely adventurous and proved that the Bering Strait was not the only way to cross the oceans to the Western Hemisphere. Most certainly there were other adventurous souls who crossed the great seas from the Eastern Hemisphere. The Vikings come to mind, and certainly Lehi's family out of Jerusalem could have made it to the new world by crossing the sea, and so they did just as it was recorded in the Book of Mormon.

In the book "America B.C.", as noted above, the author shows several pages of Micmac Algonquian Indian hieroglyphs side by side with Egyptian hieroglyphs depicting words that are either identical or very similar for the same word in both languages. This Micmac writing was in use by the Indians before 1738 when Father Abbe' Maillard adopted these hieroglyphs to communicate with the Micmac indians. Studies show several thousand Micmac hieroglyphs were modeled after the Egyptian hieroglyphs. How did Native Americans with a supposed primitive nomad Asian ancestry accidentally come up with a parallel ancient Egyptian like written language?

It wasn't the Spanish explorers who brought all these intriguing Middle Eastern cultural evidences to America, nor did the Spanish build great cities and pyramids in a Middle Eastern style in the jungles of the Western Hemisphere. "Native American" is a very generalized term for many different, highly varied groups of people who have inhabited North, Central, and South America since ancient times, and only a fool would suggest that they are a homogeneous ethnic group, all of whom came from Asia, and then coincidently developed a parallel Middle Eastern stylized pyramid culture and civilization in the Western Hemisphere.

*   *   *

Elder Dallin H. Oaks recalled his own experience at BYU:

"Here [at BYU] I was introduced to the idea that the Book of Mormon is not a history of all of the people who have lived on the continents of North and South America in all ages of the earth. Up to that time, I had assumed that it was. If that were the claim of the Book of Mormon, any piece of historical, archaeological, or linguistic evidence to the contrary would weigh in against the Book of Mormon, and those who rely exclusively on scholarship would have a promising position to argue.

In contrast, if the Book of Mormon only purports to be an account of a few peoples who inhabited a portion of the Americas during a few millennia in the past, the burden of argument changes drastically. It is no longer a question of all versus none; it is a question of some versus none. In other words, in the circumstance I describe, the opponents of historicity must prove that the Book of Mormon has no historical validity for any peoples who lived in the Americas in a particular time frame, a notoriously difficult exercise."

*　　*　　*

There are dozens of phrases in the Book of Mormon, which seem worded in a very awkward way, even grammatically incorrect. Critics have mocked this bad grammar without realizing that expert linguists; such as John A. Tvedtnes, Richard Grant, and James A. Carroll, have shown that these awkward phrases make perfect sense when translated back into Hebrew. Many of the English sentences in the Book of Mormon, that an English teacher would be highly critical of, are perfectly acceptable in Hebrew sentence structure, and so they do now appear to be a surprisingly close literal translation.

Brian D. Stubbs, one of the few linguists working with both the Indian Uto-Aztecan languages and the Hebrew Semitic languages, says that the ancient American Uto-Aztecan language "as a language family exhibits more similarities with Hebrew than could be attributed to coincidence; nevertheless, that Hebrew element is obviously mixed with other language elements very different from Hebrew." However, he has found over one thousand similarities with the Hebrew language that cannot be explained away as just mere chance or coincidence.

Many linguistic experts are often surprised and even amazed at the Semitic character of Joseph Smith's translation as they observe the obvious Hebraic language roots of the Book of Mormon, just another fascinating evidence to support it authenticity.

*　　*　　*

ANCIENT RECORDS OF THE AMERICAN INDIANS BEFORE JOSEPH SMITH AND THE BOOK OF MORMON

Milton R. Hunter, Conference Report, April 1955, p.103

"The important question for our consideration, however, is: Are there any important documents available which were written by the Indians prior to the publishing of the Book of Mormon which furnish evidence that these people had traditions which came down from their ancestors to the effect that their progenitors at a certain time in the distant past had possessed an important, sacred, religious book, which book could be identified as the Book of Mormon?

I shall answer that question in the affirmative. Yes, we do have some very important documents which were written between two and three hundred years prior to the publishing of the Book of Mormon which make the claim that many years ago the ancestors of the American Indians possessed an important, sacred book. These writings are so explicit that one could easily believe that the ancient records spoken of by the Indian writers are the same records as the ones from which the Book of Mormon was translated by the Prophet.

The first of these Indian writings of great significance, which shall be referred to, is the Works of Ixtlilxochitl, written by an Indian of the royal family in Mexico approximately 1600 A.D. In these writings he accounts the history, traditions, and religious beliefs of his people from the time of the migration of the first group from the Tower of Babel—continuing with the emigrations from over the sea of two other groups—and on down to the Spanish conquest.

The second example, which I shall give of an early Indian document, which contains numerous, marvelous evidences sustaining the claims made by the Book of Mormon, is known today as the Popol Vuh."

(Popol Vuh, The Sacred Book of the Ancient Quiche-Maya, (Eng. tr. by Delia Goetz and Sylvan G. Morley, Norman, Oklahoma, 1950), pp. 1-767.)

"The original manuscript was written in the Quiché language by a Quiché-Maya Indian in faraway Guatemala, Central America, nearly three hundred years before the Prophet Joseph Smith published the account translated from the Nephites' records. Between the years 1554 and 1558 A.D., an Indian at Chichicastenango, Guatemala wrote what has become accepted by scholars as a very important and unusual document in which he delineates the mythology, beliefs, and traditions of his people. The Quiché-Maya Indian author claimed that there was a prevalent tradition among his people that his ancestors in the distant past had at one time possessed an important, religious sacred book which had disappeared being had no more by his people, and so he wrote his manuscript to replace that lost book.

(Milton R. Hunter, Conference Report, April 1955, p.105)

*　　*　　*

Lord Kingsborough, an heir to an Irish Earl and an antiquarian in the 1800's, wrote in volume IV of his *Antiquities of Mexico*, that he had found so many examples of parallel Biblical stories among the Indians, which he had studied, that he came to the following conclusion:

"It is unnecessary to attempt in this place to trace out any further scriptural analogies in the traditions and mythology of the New

World, since the coincidences which have already been mentioned are sufficiently strong to warrant the conclusion that the Indians, at a period long antecedent to the arrival of the Spaniards in America, were acquainted with a portion at least of the Old Testament," (page 409)

*   *   *

This author is personally acquainted with a return missionary who served an LDS mission in the country of Panama in Central America among the Cuna Indians who live off the coast of Panama on the San Blas Islands. They have had little contact with white civilization, even in this day and age. These secluded Indian people not only have highly developed metallurgy skills in gold jewelry, and a pre-Columbian writing system, but my missionary friend testifies that they will often happily recount their ancient and traditional oral stories for visitors, which seem to have come right out of the Old Testament.

With all these evidences at hand, it is very reasonable to believe that some Native American people actually did have in their possession Bible stories before the arrival of the Spaniards to the Western Hemisphere. So how did they come by these Bible stories? Is it reasonable to believe that these Bible stories came originally from the Plates of Brass mentioned in the Book of Mormon, and then have been handed down for centuries through their primitive writing system and or by oral tradition? It seems very logical to believe that this is just the case.

*   *   *

Expert linguists have examined and analyzed the Book of Mormon carefully, and concluded that it is the work of many authors with different writing styles and that a single author could not have wrote it.

"Critics say that Joseph Smith fraudulently wrote the B of M himself. Scholarly analysis of the writing style (some even by computers) shows many authors wrote it; authors with a significant background in Semitic culture and writing styles. This would be virtually impossible for an uneducated farm boy to mimic." (see http://www.jefflindsay.com/BMEvidences.shtml)

*   *   *

Even every-day normal readers of the Book of Mormon have noticed the differences in writing styles in different parts of the Book of Mormon. Joseph Smith would had to have been much more than a literary genius to put together a fake book with so many evidences of multiple ancient authors.

There are far too many things in the Book of Mormon that absolutely cannot be explained away as the fabrication of Joseph Smith's mind and a product of his formal fifth grade education, even though he was obviously very intelligent. There's a great deal in this book that cannot have been put together by blind luck or just the happy coincidences of a fraudulent perpetrator. In the final analysis, the great spiritual knowledge, the religious truths, and the devout wisdom that comes out of the Book of Mormon, could only of come from a divinely wise and omniscient source who over a period of a thousands of years inspired his ancient prophets to write the history and wisdom that they recorded in the Book of Mormon.

*   *   *

In addition, many early converts during the infant days of the Church of Jesus Christ, also bore their own solid rock testimonies.

While traveling on the Erie Canal, Parley P. Pratt, a prominent apostle in the early days of the church, was first introduced to the Book of Mormon by a Baptist Deacon named Hamblin. Parley was serving as a Campbellite minister after hearing the preaching of Sidney Rigdon. He relates his experience with the book of Mormon upon first reading it;

"I opened it with eagerness and read its title page. I then read the testimony of several witnesses in relation to the manner of its being found and translated. After this I commenced its contents by course. I read all day; eating was a burden, I had no desire for food; sleep was a burden when the night came, for I preferred reading to sleep. As I read, the Spirit of the Lord was upon me, and I knew and comprehended that the book was true, as plainly and manifestly as a man comprehends and know that he exists. My joy was now full . . ." (Autobiography of Parley P. Pratt, pp. 36-37, 40) (History of the Church, Vol.1, p.118, Footnotes)

Samuel H. Smith was the Prophet's younger brother and the first member of the newly budding Mormon church to be called as a missionary. Reverend John Green, an unintentional convert to the Book of Mormon, was a Methodist preacher whose wife was persuaded to read the Book of Mormon by Elder Smith. When the preacher discovered his wife's Book of Mormon, he grabbed it out of her hands and said that he would prove to her that it was the work of Satan in the first two pages. He read two pages and then two more, and soon had read the whole book without eating or sleeping. He fully intended to disprove the Book of Mormon, but only succeeded in converting himself, just by reading its intriguing pages and experiencing the special spirit that accompanies this unusual book. (Jack H. West—"The Trial of the Stick of Joseph" p. 60 *

BOOK OF MORMON WITNESSES

Encyclopedia of Mormonism: "The testimonies of the Three and Eight Witnesses balance the supernatural and the natural, the one stressing the angel and heavenly voice, the other the existence of a tangible record on gold plates. To the end of their lives, each of the Three said he had seen the plates, and each of the Eight insisted that he had handled them. Most of the Eight and all of the Three Witnesses reiterated their Book of Mormon testimonies just before death. Together with Joseph Smith they fulfill Nephi's prophecy: "They shall testify to the truth of the book and the things therein" (2 Ne. 27:12). Encyclopedia of Mormonism, Vol.1, BOOK OF MORMON WITNESSES

*   *   *

BOOK OF MORMON: THE BIGGER PICTURE

CONCLUSION OR JUST THE BEGINNING

The Book of Mormon will always be controversial because it does have a unique "birth" and a unparalleled history, and thus it effects a strong emotional response from all people who become acquainted with it; whether that response be utter disdain and the unfounded belief that it is a fraudulent religious perpetration, or the complete opposite; the sincere belief that it is truly an ancient record and spiritual word brought forth by an angel of God for the good of mankind. There doesn't seem to be any neutral opinions in regards to this fascinating and unique book.

The Prophet Joseph Smith said about the Book of Mormon: "I told the brethren that the Book of Mormon was the most correct book on earth, and the keystone of our religion, and a man would get nearer to God by abiding by its precepts, than by any other book." Every prophet of the LDS church since that time has tried to emphasize that very idea and that great truth.

Since the Book of Mormon was published in 1830, a great many anti-Mormon distracters have desperately tried to find a "chink" in its authenticity. Its integrity has withstood the storms and spears of all attackers, while genuine investigators and those with an open mind and heart have been enthralled and spellbound by its spirit and message. Such is the case with hundreds of thousands of converts each year, who bare a wide variety of testimonies and personal stories and testify to the spirit of truth that they felt while reading the Book of Mormon.

The Book of Mormon has influenced and changed the lives of literally millions of people around the world. They have found it to be a truly authentic record of an ancient people, and that it is now divinely brought forth and translated in modern times for the benefit of the descendants of the Lehi and the entire world. To those who sincerely and prayerfully read its pages, it truly carries with it a very special spirit like no other book, and like no other record in history.

*   *   *

"And now, my beloved brethren, all those who are of the house of Israel, and all ye ends of the earth, I speak unto you as the voice of one crying from the dust: Farewell until that great day shall come."
2 Nephi 33:13